A Ghost in the Middle Kingdom

a Memoir

Anna Keibler

Black Rose Writing | Texas

©2025 by Anna Keibler
All rights reserved. No part of this book may be reproduced, stored in a retrieval system or transmitted in any form or by any means without the prior written permission of the publishers, except by a reviewer who may quote brief passages in a review to be printed in a newspaper, magazine or journal.

The author grants the final approval for this literary material.

First printing

Some names and identifying details may have been changed to protect the privacy of individuals.

ISBN: 978-1-68513-629-1
LIBRARY OF CONGRESS CONTROL NUMBER:2025931107
PUBLISHED BY BLACK ROSE WRITING
www.blackrosewriting.com

Printed in the United States of America
Suggested Retail Price (SRP) $19.95

A Ghost in the Middle Kingdom is printed in Minion Pro

*As a planet-friendly publisher, Black Rose Writing does its best to eliminate unnecessary waste to reduce paper usage and energy costs, while never compromising the reading experience. As a result, the final word count vs. page count may not meet common expectations.

Dedicated to Micah, who caught me when I fell and encouraged me to write my truth.

A Ghost in the Middle Kingdom

Prologue

I woke early in the morning between warm layers of cotton pads, a beer bottle beside me still cold to the touch. I was in this canvas tent alone, the coal-burning stove roaring in the center of the structure. Its six-foot vent pipe barely stuck out of the hole in the tent ceiling, just high enough to keep the smoke from pouring back inside. I didn't bother changing my clothes. I had only been in them for a day beforehand, and my clean outfits were in short supply. The tent was tall enough for me to stand up, but being that I'm only five-foot-two, I doubt the average woman could say the same. I shifted my clothes around my body to appear a bit more presentable, then I listened, waiting for what seemed like a reasonable amount of time.

Nobody came, and I heard nothing. Slowly, I pushed aside the thick, padded door that hung in the tent's entryway and stepped outside.

The bright mountain sunlight beamed on my face in a blinding aura against an azure sky. I was camped at approximately 19,000 feet altitude, deep in the Qilian mountains of the Qinghai-Tibetan Plateau. The short blades of the sedge grasses were all yellow this time of year but still covered everything in sight in a blanket of color that felt drab yet promising. I walked to the edge of the small eight-foot cliff near the camp's position and stood staring at the point where the horizon met the sky.

I slowly turned my head from side to side, drinking up as much of the view as I could with every small turn of my neck. The mountains rose up on either side of me, but the view ahead of me was of the rolling foothills that met with the alpine steppe plains below. I looked from the sky to the ground and realized I was the first foreigner to set foot in this very spot, likely ever in the history of modern China. The magic and beauty of the scene overwhelmed me, as if I were the luckiest person alive. I was truly on an adventure, the stuff of my dreams—but I had not yet found the man I sought, and law forbid my presence here. Oh, what a shame this came on the heels of what felt like torture! How did I end up sinking so low?

Chapter 1

During the summer between middle school and high school, I thought it would be a good idea to put my hair in dreadlocks. I was engrossed in discovering my identity and spirituality and fancied myself a proper hippy. I studied books about neo-Paganism. I became a priestess, and I decided to go on a journey of spiritual introspection, like so many hippies before me, through my hair. The locks were like little radio antennas into my soul, each one decidedly representing a milestone I would have to undergo in order to become "whole." I had thirty-three dreadlocks total. That meant thirty-three milestones, although I had no idea when those milestones might come.

I made these dreadlocks by first sectioning my hair, then backcombing it from end-to-end. I twisted and rubbed and rolled each lock for hours on end. If my body had a moment to be still, my hands were in my hair. Later, a family friend who had also once had dreadlocks taught me a new method of getting my hair to tighten, one passed down to her by a senior hippy at a drum circle. She taught me how to take my locks by the ends and rip them down the center until a tiny ball of knotted hair formed at the base of the scalp. From there, continuous ripping and regathering would lead to bigger knots that would grow on top of each other as the process continued. It hurt, but by the end of the day, my pathetic, floppy baby dreads had transformed into thick knots that poked out of my head like a cartoon cat who just had a bomb explode in his face.

By the time I started high school, the locks had tightened and matted themselves into mature looking dreads that no longer needed constant attention and rubbing. Occasionally, I would rip at the ends of the locks that still had a bit of loose hair, a soothing practice that I would continue for the next decade. But I have grown a considerable amount since my teenage years, and although I miss my dreadlocks dearly, they truly weren't meant for my hair type. I appropriated this hairstyle as a part of my identity, and action I wouldn't repeat today. Still, my dreadlocks were a large defining point of who I was in China.

The teenage version of me took great delight in discovering who I was with dreadlocks. I dyed them various shades of teals and pinks, bleached them bright blonde, and darkened them to raven black. I eventually settled on fuchsia as a permanent look, with only a few locks dyed completely, a handful of locks partially dyed, and most locks retaining their natural shade of dirty blonde. They grew quickly, and by the time I reached China in 2011, some even reached my waistline.

My dreadlocks were an amazing conversation point in China. Most locals had never seen hair like that before, and everyone wanted to touch and pull. I kept the locks gathered high on my head in a ponytail, fixed in a position that caused them to first sprout up like a lively spider plant before drooping back down across my shoulders. Flying both domestically and internationally, I was asked more than once to take this ponytail down so the security agents could check my hair for contraband. I didn't mind the groping hands that came for my hair, though. I was glad to talk about it, and was absolutely thrilled every time I was asked the question, "Were you born like that?" By the time I left for China in 2011, they were a key part of both my persona and spirituality, and I don't know if the journey would have been the same without them.

Lucky for me, I had an advantage going to China that most other foreigners didn't—I'd studied Chinese in high school and could hold a minor conversation with anyone who wanted to talk. In fact, I'd been to China before, too. My last two years of high school were spent at a publicly funded charter school that boarded three hundred of Indiana's highest achieving students from around the state. My previous school was very rural, with just over a thousand combined middle and high school students. I was bored there and miserable with few friends. When the invitation to apply to the Indiana Academy for Science, Mathematics, and Humanities reached my doorstep, I jumped at the opportunity to attend. The academy boasted a wide array of language options for their students, including Russian, Latin, and Chinese. Most students seemed to split between Spanish and Japanese, the latter thanks to the degree of popularity of anime among nerdy youths. I, however, on my quest to be just a bit different from everybody else, opted for Chinese.

I spent two years taking Chinese language courses from Dr. Min Zhang, who originally hailed from Wuhan, Hebei province. She had lived in the US for decades, but her slight Chinese accent was intoxicating to listen to, and I tried to gobble up as much information as she would sling at us. She gave me the Chinese name of *AnNa*. It was a transliteration of my name, but *An* is a common Chinese surname meaning "Peace," so it was a much better name than other western transliterations.

I was a mediocre Chinese student. The class was right after lunch, and the school had me worn so mentally ragged that I would often retreat back to my dormitory after the hour break just to catch ten minutes of precious sleep before heading out to the start of afternoon classes. The distance-learning room where Chinese class was held every Tuesday and Thursday was always overly warm and made my eyelids heavy. I sat in the back of the classroom next to my learning partner, Jane, where we toyed with fun pronunciations and made pictures out of the Chinese characters.

We were attentive, though, and eager to stay awake for Thursday's culture lessons. Here, we would learn to sing traditional Chinese folk songs, watch old Chinese movies, and eat authentic Chinese food. I fell in love with the movie "Raise the Red Lantern," a story about a young female scholar who gives up her dream of university to become a concubine. She is eventually driven mad and resigns to her fate of wandering her small compound with only her madness to keep her company. It remains my favorite Chinese film to this day. Furthermore, during the first year of lessons, the school organized a two-week trip to China as part of the pre-summer curriculum. My parents somehow scrounged up the funds for me to go, eager to give me such a rare opportunity.

China was exquisite. We feasted at fine dumpling houses in Beijing, rolled down the steep ramps of the Great Wall, took boat rides down the soft flowing rivers of Guilin, stood in awe of the terra-cotta warriors, and learned to barter in Shanghai. The whole country was beautiful, the food was amazing, and everything was fresh and exciting. What I hadn't realized, however, was that in planning this trip, Dr. Zhang really had taken us to the best places that a tour group could see. Our experience was tailored to us as Westerners. We were shepherded to China's beauty and shielded from its less than pleasant truths. But still, the experience stuck in my soul, and I vowed to one day return to this enchanted land.

Unfortunately, I lost most of my Chinese after graduating high school. It wasn't offered at my university, and I had nobody to practice with except myself. So, I let it slip away. I'd convinced myself that becoming an astronautical engineer would be the quickest way to become an actual astronaut, and I was dead set on going to Mars. My engineering dreams soon fell through, however, as I realized that I just wasn't interested in building things, or coding things, or really, even attending classes. I was burnt out on college life, and it was at this point that my bipolar disorder began to bloom.

Living off campus, I swung into a deep depression that centered on a developed eating disorder. I'd quit going to classes and wore the same outfit to work every day. I would then rapid-cycle into hypomania and begin making very unwise choices that involved buying various creatures that I had no business taking care of. A bunny. A kitten. A pair of hermit crabs. A green anole that bit me before escaping. When I eventually came to the conclusion that I could devote neither the time, energy, nor funding to these creatures, I would desperately seek out new homes for them and cry myself to sleep at night wracked with guilt. I didn't know what was happening to me or why I felt the way I did. The thought of being bipolar wouldn't even be on my radar until 2018, almost ten years later.

I don't know if my parents knew what was going on. I was six hours away from them, still within the state of Indiana but far enough away for them to worry. I have a suspicion that, while they didn't know any specifics, they could tell I wasn't doing well. One day, my father made the drive up to Lafayette just to visit me. No particular reason in mind, just to catch dinner. I don't know if he was coming up to try to save me or if it was just something that had been on his mind, but he planted the seed of transferring universities in my brain. That seed sprouted overnight, transforming into vines that consumed me. All I could focus on was getting away, getting home. By the end of the semester, I was officially enrolled at the University of Louisville and moved back to my childhood home in Milltown over Christmas break.

To my delight, the University of Louisville had a Chinese program. My advisor placed me in the intermediate language course based on my transcripts, although I was entering class during the second semester and quickly fell behind. After all, I'd missed a whole previous semester of information. I decided I didn't have it in me to try to catch up and let myself fail the course. Instead, I focused on an array of electives I'd chosen while still trying to decide my new major: Women in Literature, Religion in Asia, and Environmental Policy.

One day, after visiting a professor's office, I noticed a poster calling for students interested in an exchange program with a Chinese university. "Study abroad in China!" I remember making the decision instantly that this was the path I should take. I was a very lucky student, after all, because my parents were both employed by the university, meaning they and their dependents were granted tuition remission. This meant the tuition to study abroad was covered by the remission program, and all I needed to pay for were plane tickets and on-campus boarding. I was sold.

My family and friends were skeptical, though. I was engaged at this point, to a man five years my senior, but there was much trouble in our paradise. We had been unable to afford our city loft apartment next to the university and ended up moving in with my grandmother about thirty minutes away. He proposed to me in his bathrobe, with a card he was saving for Christmas. It was supposed to be romantic, but instead he presented me with a sterling silver engagement ring one week before the holiday and told me, "I might as well give this to you now." I accepted and pretended to be happy, convincing myself that fairytale engagements were just for movies and I should consider myself lucky that he asked at all. He wasn't thrilled about my drive to go to China, but since it was only for a semester, he promised to wait patiently for my return. My parents never said a negative word to me, although my mother later told me that after I'd boarded the plane, my father sat in his garden for many hours until bursting into the house, frantic that they'd let their daughter go sauntering off to a communist country. While others had their concerns, I wasn't bothered by the political situation of the Middle Kingdom.

Chapter 2

I landed in the city of Jinan, Shandong Province at midnight on February 11, 2011. Situated approximately halfway between Beijing and Shanghai, I chose Jinan precisely because I'd never heard of it before. The other cities to choose from were massive, but Jinan was considered small. With a population of only seven million spread between the city proper and the outlying countryside, it was considered a small Tier 3 Chinese city. Today, Jinan is a Tier 2 city with over nine million people, and the city has almost tripled in area. Back then, the city was still a lazy city. That is, the people prided themselves on being unhurried, on the buildings being small, and on the sense of freedom everyone felt while living in such a geographically large area with such few people.

Jinan was known as the "City of Springs," named after the seventy-two artesian springs that flowed through the city. The city parks and gardens were lush and full of life, each spring teeming with magnificent giant koi and flowering lotuses. Forested mountains bordered the city to the south, and the Yellow River roared past the city in the north. In the center of the city, a large man-made lake boasted tranquil views and rising pagodas. Temples littered the city, and the intact hutongs, the traditional narrow alleyways lined with courtyard houses, were filled with lively vendors selling practically anything you could imagine.

My university, Shandong University, was located in the LiCheng District towards the eastern edge of the city. On the night of my arrival, a student ambassador named Chen from the international program met me at the airport. His friend had a friend who had a car, and they stuffed my belongings—a large hiking backpack filled to the brim and a fifty-pound suitcase—into the trunk before insisting I take the front seat. I reached for the seatbelt, only to find it had been removed. This was a common practice, especially in back seats where they were often tucked back in between the cushions to provide a more comfortable sitting space with little confinement. Safety be damned. We reached the university's international student building a little before two a.m. where Chen dropped me off and wished me luck before vanishing into the night.

The front reception of the international student building had no English speakers. In fact, they didn't even know I was coming. It took them about thirty minutes to find my information, then another thirty minutes to unlock my room in the dormitories upstairs. When I finally walked into my room, I gasped. The light was hanging from the ceiling by an exposed wire. The water pipes and electricity conduits were all *outside* the walls, which themselves were full of various cracks and peeling paint. In the bathroom, no separation existed between the toilet and the shower, and I couldn't tell if what lay on my bed was meant to be used as a large towel or a small blanket. That night, I used it as a blanket but found it far too scratchy and later used it as a towel instead.

I was shocked and couldn't believe what a dingy little room I'd been given. How could this be right? Why was the place so outdated? Was it even safe? Why did it look like something I'd seen in a sad movie? I tried to put these thoughts out of my head as I fell asleep that night, exhausted from the twenty-seven-hour journey. Things didn't improve the next day, either. When I walked outside the student building, I found the roads coated in dust. Chen retrieved me for a trip to the grocery store, and I couldn't help but feel aghast at the amount of trash that littered the streets. The cars never stopped honking, dodging and weaving in between the people, bicycles, motorbikes, and carts that crossed their paths. The further we got from the university grounds, the denser the afternoon population became, and I realized for the first time just how far away home was and how odd of a sight I must have been.

I was overweight when I went to China, around two hundred pounds on a five-foot-two frame. Most people in China were far, far smaller than I was, and my weight was something that strangers had no problem pointing out to me. I was also simply not used to all the walking that was required. The big grocery and department store was less than a mile away from campus, but Chen liked to walk fast. I huffed along behind, trying my best to keep up with both my pace and the conversation we were trying to make. It was then that I first heard a stranger on the sidewalk call out, "*Yang guizi!*" in my direction, meaning "foreign ghost" or "foreign devil." Chen's cheeks reddened in embarrassment as he explained the phrase. Chen spoke nearly perfect English but still felt it wasn't good enough and was eager for the opportunity to improve. I'd been called a lot worse things than a *yang guizi*, though, and was warned before coming that not everyone would be thrilled about my foreign presence in the country, especially as an American.

Chen helped me carry my grocery bags back to campus then treated me to my first meal since landing—chicken dumplings. The thought of meaty, juicy chicken inside a dumpling sounded like just the type of heaven I needed… except they were terrible! The meat inside was chicken livers and gizzards, which just was not my taste. Growing up with vegetarian parents, I simply was not used to eating the non-meaty bits of an animal. I could hardly even handle eating anything with bones. No chicken wings or T-bone steaks for me, thank you.

Perhaps the most jarring piece of cultural division was the general lack of empathy towards anyone who was not your friend. Once you made a friend in China, you've made a friend for life, and those friends will move heaven and earth for you at a moment's notice. The same cannot be said for strangers. Strangers do not matter; they are but another meaty body standing in the way. If you get injured on the streets in China, do not expect anyone to intervene on your behalf. Onlookers will gather, cell phones in hand to record the incident, but they will not step in to help you. This, of course, is generalized information. I have met a few people in China who were willing to help a fellow stranger, but they were very few and far between.

By the end of my first twenty-four hours in China, I was ready to go home. My feet were blistered. I hadn't had a decent meal since the international flight. Everything was dusty, dirty, and decrepit. This was a far cry from the China I met in high school. Where was the beauty? Where were the pleasantries? If only I had known how much comfort I'd be giving up by going on this adventure, I would have opted for a larger city like Beijing or Shanghai! I didn't even have a pillow or blanket. Chen was nice, but he still had his own college student life to live and couldn't babysit me like a scared child. I hated it there. I immediately began researching how to transfer to a larger city. I thought a more populous area would be more like the cities back home, and if only I could transfer within a few weeks, I wouldn't miss much of class and could easily catch up.

After a few weeks of living in China, I learned that in terms of both individual and collective behavior, it was a fallacy to believe China's bigger cities would be any different than Jinan. The trash and exposed pipes were something I'd encounter no matter what city I was in, and in reality, I was very lucky to be in a city as romantically lazy as Jinan. It took me about a month to abandon the notion of leaving Jinan, and it took three months before I fell in love with where I was.

Thankfully, by the end of my first week in China, I had integrated into a wonderful group of international friends. I was the only American in the entire dormitory and the only person with dreadlocks. I experienced a bit of flack for being American, and several of my peers were not shy in the least about voicing their disdain for my home country. I agreed with most of what was said, though. Our policies have hurt many people. Regardless, my core group of friends was unbothered by who I was or what I looked like and instead took great delight in learning that red solo cups can actually be bought in grocery stores and are not just a Hollywood prop to symbolize an alcoholic beverage. My friends came from all over the globe—Brazil, Canada, France, Germany, Russia, Denmark, South Africa, Lesotho, Saudi Arabia, Pakistan, Spain, Korea—and we banded together like we'd known each other our whole lives. A special sort of bonding takes place when you've all uprooted yourselves to go to China, and I quickly found there was much more to the city than what initially met my eyes.

The experienced foreigners, the ones who had already been at ShanDa (shorthand for Shandong University) for a year or two, were eager to show us the best places to eat, take us down to the bustling night markets, and reveal to us the tranquilities of the city's springs and parks. We also liked to party, and we soon discovered an array of bars and clubs that stayed open almost all night long. We experienced the pure, unadulterated joy that came from sitting on tiny stools at tiny tables set up in the streets and sidewalks for barbeque. Restaurants would skewer bits of mutton and garlic, coat them in a special cumin rub, and grill them by the dozens. Complete with a crate of warm Qingdao beer and time to kill, we often stayed in the barbeque quarters for entire evenings.

I took up smoking in China, too. It came about when our friend group decided to spend our days off for the Tomb-Sweeping Festival touring the city and suburbs of Hangzhou, an area south of us that was renowned for its beautiful scenic gardens and waterways. We took a day trip to Nanjing to visit the Memorial Hall for the Nanjing Massacre, and in the evening we ended up at a tiny hole-in-the-wall bar aimed at foreigners. I bought a bottle of liquor for our table, and the drinking games commenced. Seeing we were a group of outsiders, however, it didn't take long for the local Nanjing foreigners to give in to their curiosity and inquire as to who we were and where we'd come from. This was not in a defensive manner, mind you. The most experienced foreigners in China always welcomed other foreigners with open arms, eager for shared experiences and new tales of adventure.

A group of Saudi Arabians had brought their own shisha, a form of tobacco, and urged us to partake. I had never smoked anything before, not even a joint, but I took up the mouthpiece of the hookah and inhaled deeply. The smoke was surprisingly smooth, tasted fruity, and filled my lungs with a sensation of fullness. I exhaled a large puff of smoke that hung in the air like a raincloud. The experience was surprisingly pleasant. We poured a round for our new friends, and we all threw back a shot. Most of the Saudis drank alcohol in China. Some even ate non-halal meat. They were always well off financially, thanks to large monthly stipends from their government, and they lived in China like kings. Of course, the smoking, drinking, and random sex would all stop before returning home, but for the few years they stayed in China, nothing was off the table.

By the end of the hour, the liquor and the shisha were both gone, our lungs coated in nicotine and our bellies full of happiness, but I wanted more. I begged my friend, Dee, for one of her cigarettes. "Just to try it," I said. It didn't take much convincing, but she told me she would feel bad if she was the reason I started smoking. After that, I was hooked. I remember buying my first pack of cigarettes after returning home from Hangzhou, choosing a pack of the red and brown TaiShan brand. I didn't know if they were any good. I just liked the way the box looked. At first, I could barely make it through a whole cigarette and only smoked outside. It took me a week to finish a pack.

If you're a man in China, smoking is as common as breathing. If you're a woman who smokes, you're a "bad girl." I was forgiven for being such a bad girl, however, due to my status as a foreigner. I found the same social stigma didn't apply to me, and most of the men were actually very happy to smoke with a foreign woman. In China, cigarettes are a shared experience. When gathering with friends, one should always offer his or her own cigarettes up for being smoked first. When seated for dinner, one should always place his or her own cigarettes on the table so others can experiment with new brands. Always light the cigarette for your friends, guests, or those above you in status. If your cigarette is being lit, gently tap the lighter holder's hand to indicate you're finished with the flame.

Most smokers held off on smoking in places like department stores and small businesses, but restaurants, offices, homes, and any public area were considered free game. If you didn't like smoke, the onus was on you to get out of the way. Furthermore, cigarettes in China were cheap. A low-quality brand cost a mere five yuan, or less than one US dollar. The fanciest brands cost up to a hundred yuan per pack. But most brands cost between ten and twenty yuan, or about two dollars and fifty cents USD. So, it was incredibly easy to smoke in China, and the glowing ember of a cigarette became congruent with making memories.

Chapter 3

By the end of my first three months in Jinan, I knew I didn't want to leave. The city had grown on me immensely, and I even found the dusty sidewalks and chipping paint to be a little charming. Every day felt like a new adventure. There was always something new to do, some new place to explore, some new friend to make. And we made lots of friends. In a country with over a billion people, it's hard not to make friends, even boyfriends. When I told my fiancé I wouldn't be coming home at the end of the semester, opting instead to extend my stay for another six months, he was supportive but tired. He just wanted me to come home. But I wasn't ready. In fact, I wasn't ready to get married, either. The whole world had just opened up to me, and it would be a shame to pin myself down to someone at only nineteen years old. He had secretly started meeting up with a female coworker, too. We ended our engagement right before Christmas of that year. We were both more than ready for the split, and it made me feel so free. I wasted no time in letting my eyes wander to new romantic interests, and I soon met a local man named Zhen.

Zhen was a stylist at a local barbershop just down the street from the university. My Bahrani friend, Muqtada, who always had very stylish hair, gave him my cell phone number after Zhen asked if he knew of any other foreigners he could be friends with. Muqtada was unfamiliar with Western social etiquette in terms of knowing when and when not to give numbers out to people, especially giving the phone number of a woman out to a strange man. Still, he knew I was friendly and that my Chinese was decent, so he sent Zhen my way. At first, I was reluctant to respond to texts from a stranger, but after speaking with Muqtada about the whole ordeal, he confirmed that Zhen was a nice person truly interested in meeting more foreign friends. So, I indulged him.

It was great language practice. Zhen and I texted constantly. It was all in Chinese, but luckily, I had a small Chinese-English dictionary that allowed me to look up new and unfamiliar characters using stroke order. Eventually, I began to invite him out to the bars with us. I could tell he was a little uncomfortable being around so many people he couldn't understand. I told him the feeling was very familiar. We began dating a few weeks later. Our relationship was casual, but fulfilling, and as my conversational Chinese gradually improved, Zhen became a lifelong friend. Eventually, I would move in with Zhen after my remaining semester at the university ended, deciding not to reenroll. He had two children from a previous relationship and brought them from the countryside to live in our apartment. His nine-year-old girl was quiet and reserved with her hair cut in a short bob. She was diligent in her studies and well-mannered in front of adults. He also had a five-year-old boy who was spirited and feisty. He practiced kung fu moves in the living room almost every evening, knocking over Zhen's empty beer bottles from the coffee table with the thrust of his arms. This always ended in intense scolding, much to the delight of his sister.

By the time I lived with Zhen and his family, we weren't dating anymore. Our relationship lasted a month before realizing we were just too different for each other, but we harbored no ill will against one another, and the living arrangement benefitted us both. I gained invaluable experience living with a Chinese family and integrated myself into Chinese culture as deeply as possible. Zhen's mother even made me a thick cotton marital quilt—not because I was getting married, but because I needed something hefty, wide, and warm to sleep under. She had stitched the two-inch thick blanket by hand, and it is the one item I wish I could have brought back home with me. Leaving it behind brought tears to my eyes.

In the months before moving in with Zhen, I had been approached by an English-speaking university worker about taking up a job offer as an English teacher for a high school in a nearby town called Tai'An. With finals complete and our summer break ahead of us, most native English speakers were able to snag a part-time position as an English teacher for a private language school. These language schools held classes in the evening, after students were released from their daily classes at regular school. Most students were elementary aged, with middle and high school students making up a small population of learners. Most high schoolers were too busy focusing on college entrance exams, even as freshmen, to find the time to attend after-school classes. Of course, for us foreign college students, landing one of these jobs was very illegal. Our student visas were good for one thing and one thing only—attending university. We were not to hold jobs while on a student visa, even part-time positions. Those were reserved for individuals with business visas. You needed a bachelor's degree and a signed offer letter for that, though, and it was much easier for language schools to pull their foreign teachers off the streets.

I wouldn't be at ShanDa anymore, but my student visa still granted me almost another year's time in the country. I decided a job would be a nice way to stay in China, especially Jinan, without having to leave home to get a new visa. What I wasn't told at the time was that I would never qualify for a working visa to begin with, since I had no bachelor's degree. Still, I signed up with the high school to teach an American culture class over the summer for students who wanted to attend American universities, and come fall, I was teaching SAT prep. Tai'An was situated only an hour away from Jinan by slow train, nestled beneath the looming Mount Tai, one of China's tallest mountains. My recruiter and manager, who was the head of the foreign English teaching department, put me up in a very nice apartment above a hotel. It was close enough to the school that I could walk there in an hour. By this time, I had become an avid walker, and I welcomed the stroll to and from the school every day. I taught for a year, guiding students through practice quizzes, essay writing, and calculus in English. I would spend the weekdays in Tai'An, and come Friday night, I would hop a train back to Jinan to be with all my friends. I still kept a small loft apartment in Jinan, where I would return during the summer and winter breaks.

On these train rides, I would position myself in between the cars, where the smokers would congregate. Many of these smokers were migrant workers with standing-only tickets, also traveling between Tai'An and Jinan. They were fascinated by me and I by them. They spoke no English, but were more than happy to let me practice my Chinese with them. In fact, I owe a big part of my Chinese language skills to these men. They would chortle as I made mistakes then tenderly correct me, urging me to try again. I learned to speak like them. These train rides were better than any classroom I'd been in, and I soon picked up enough slang and colloquialism for me to sound like I could actually speak the language. However, my whole world crumbled when my visa expired.

Shortly before the next summer break, I went to my manager to let him know my visa would expire soon and that without an invitation letter from the high school, I wouldn't be able to come back and teach. In fact, I would need to leave China in order to get a new visa. And soon. My manager told me not to worry since he had connections with the Public Service Bureau and could get me a shiny new work visa just by greasing a few palms. The latter wasn't spoken but implied. In those days, every foreign school in the city had at least one illegal foreign teacher, and bribes to keep the police from raiding the facilities were expected. So, hearing that my manager could use his *guanxi*, or personal relations, to get me a visa, my mind was put at ease.

Just days before my visa expired, my manager called me with bad news. The high school was refusing to give him an invitation letter for my employment because that would be illegal. They were fine with him forging my college graduation documents but drew the line at their own involvement. For me, that meant no new visa. Furthermore, it meant I would certainly be in China illegally, at least for a few days, because there was no way I could pay for a plane ticket and arrange my departure in time. My manager had also withheld my last paycheck, stating he needed the money for the now non-existent visa. I knew that overstaying my visa could result in heavy fines and could possibly land me on a blacklist. Do not enter. Exiled from China. I could not have this happen to me. I was frantic. So, I did the only reasonable thing I could think of doing—I went to the police.

By the time I got to the Jinan PSB, my visa had officially expired. I sat down in a booth with a low-level agent, to whom I explained the situation. She put her hand up halfway through my story and told me to wait. This was above her pay grade. She referred me to a pair of detectives, who took me into a small office and closed the door. I was sitting alone, just waiting for something to happen, when suddenly my phone rang. It was my manager, and he knew I was with the police. He told me to remember he had been good to me, he had provided me with a high-paying, respectable job, paid for my apartment, and treated me to all sorts of dinners during my employment. He begged me not to turn him or the school in and to instead claim I was employed by a different school. *Remember that tiny little foreign language school in the LiXia district? The one that has nothing but illegal foreign teachers? I know you taught there for a few days. Turn them in, instead. Nothing bad will happen to you, and you'll save us both from a lot of trouble.* Involving the high school, after all, would certainly cause a lot of trouble, and I should do the right thing.

I was befuddled. How had he known I was there? It must have been through his connections with the PSB. That meant somebody called him to give him a heads up, and then he called me. I was beyond nervous, and he was right. He really had gone out of his way for me. I was good at my job, my students all excelled, and they rewarded me handsomely. I decided to do what my manager said and pretend the school that hired me was the poor, unsuspecting English training school in the LiXia district. What I told the police was simple: I had been working at the training school for a year, they told me they would provide me with a business visa, but they lied about it until my visa expired. The detectives nodded and told me not to worry. We'd get to the bottom of it all. They told me to follow them and took me to a police vehicle. Then we did something terrible. We drove to the school.

Upon our arrival, the school was closed. It wasn't time for students yet—ESL classes didn't start until after school—and since it was still mid-afternoon neither the Chinese staff nor the foreign teachers were in the building. The receptionist and a few administrators were there, however, and someone eventually let us in. The police told them to stay in the lobby, that an investigation was going on, and they had better not interfere. The detectives then pulled out a digital camera and began taking pictures. They had me lead them through the school halls to the classrooms where I had taught. I had only ever taught in one classroom before, but I stopped at two or three doors. They had me stand next to the entrance with my finger pointing at the signs on the doors indicating the students' grade level. The rainbow class was for kindergarteners. The sunny class was for second and third graders, and so on. The whole ordeal took maybe ten minutes, and I felt bad for throwing this school under the bus, but what else could I do? I'd already started down this path, and it was true the school had only illegal foreign teachers. I concluded they could simply keep paying their monthly bribes, maybe a little more this month for all the hassle, and things would go back to normal for everybody.

We got back in the detectives' car and began driving again. I wasn't sure where we were going. To my surprise, we stopped outside a high-end restaurant near my Jinan apartment. They took me inside, and the three of us sat down for an early dinner. Their treat. I felt so awkward—I had just lied to the police and here they were taking me out to dinner. Midway through the meal, one detective put his chopsticks down and looked me in the eye.

"You know, we're going to get to the bottom of this. Schools all over this city are using foreign students like cattle. They know it's illegal. Don't you worry, you did the right thing. We're going to make sure you're okay and that there's retaliation against the school."

My heart sank. I wanted to scream. I wanted to confess that everything I'd done that day was a lie. I wanted to tell them the truth, but my manager had been texting me throughout the day to make sure I was doing "the right thing," and a part of me thought my American passport would protect me. Being an American meant status in the world, right? That's what we'd always been taught in school, anyways. Of course, in China, it doesn't matter what kind of passport you have—everybody follows the same laws. And everybody gets the same punishment—unless you have money. After the meal was over, I thanked the detectives for their help. They thanked me in return and said they would look after me. "Look after a liar," I thought to myself. They told me they would meet with me again the next day, just to wait for their call.

I stayed the night in my Jinan apartment and awoke early the next day, not wanting to miss their call. It finally came in around ten a.m., with one of the detectives telling me to hurry down to the PSB as soon as possible. There had been a development, and they needed my help. I rushed to the PSB and was directed to a large office upstairs that held the desks of five special detectives. Inside, the foreign teacher manager of the little language school was standing in front of yesterday's detectives, frantically yelling. Upon hearing me enter the room, she turned around.

"Her!" she yelled. "She's lying!" Then she strode from the room.

The police officers told me to sit down. They showed me text message exchanges between her and me and said they knew I didn't work there, that I'd only filled in for a few classes a handful of times. What's more, they said, that woman I just saw lost her child yesterday. She should be at home mourning his death, but instead, she had been dragged down to the PSB because of me and my lies. They had caught me. Once I heard about this woman's dead child, I burst into tears. I cried out a line of apologies, first to the woman standing outside the room and then to the police officers. I hadn't actually worked at that school. I worked for the Tai'An high school. Looking back, I truly believe the child did not die, that it was in fact a ruse to get me to confess. They were using my emotions to get to the truth. And it worked like a charm.

Upon hearing my confession, one of the detectives sat down next to me. "If you tell us the truth right now," he said, "we can help you out of this. Tell us all the information you have, all of it this time, and you won't get into any major trouble." I agreed. Right then, my phone rang. It was my manager again! I told the detective who was calling, and he instructed me to answer, putting the call on speaker phone.

"Where are you?" my manager demanded.

"I'm at my apartment," I said.

"No, you're not! Don't lie to me! Why are you doing this?" He was frantic, and he knew where I was. Somehow, he once again knew exactly what I was doing.

The detective muttered to me in a low voice, "Don't tell him anything. Just tell him you're at home."

Then my manager said to me, using English for the first time, "You hurt me." He hung up.

I put my phone away, shaking, and the detectives ushered me to a small room with a smaller desk. I don't know whose desk it was, but it was littered with papers and folders, all strewn about the desk as if someone had been searching for a lost pen that had hidden away underneath a cluster of manilla folders. One detective sat down at the desk while the other brought in a recording device. "Tell me everything," the detective said, "and start from the beginning. Start from arriving in China." So, I told him everything I could, how I was a student at ShanDa before meeting my manager on campus. I told them my manager worked for the university full time and was working as my manager for the high school as his side gig. I told them about my apartment in Tai'An, about how I was making money hand over fist, and how that money had been withheld from me for a new visa. I gave them my manager's phone number. The detective hurriedly jotted everything down in his notebook before turning off the recording device. "Wait here," he said.

When he returned, he brought me a piece of official looking paper, fully blank except for the PSB information at the top. The paper was lined, as if it were from a notebook.

"Write it all down," he said. "Everything you told me. And it needs to be in Chinese."

I told him I didn't know how to write that well, and I certainly didn't know all the words I should use. My speaking was great, but writing an official police document was going to be a struggle. The detective told me I could use my phone as a dictionary to look up words and characters. So, I began to write. It took me three hours to write my full account, filling a page and a half. The process was long and arduous. Halfway through, the detective took me to the PSB's cafeteria for lunch. We ate in silence this time. When I'd finished writing, the detective told me to go home and wait for further instructions. Don't leave the city. Answer when called.

Three days later, I got a call from one of the detectives. He told me everything had been sorted. Thanks to my cooperation, they were able to file charges against my manager. They told me that, although I had lied to them, I was also a victim here. My manager had used me for his own gain and was raking in quite a bit of money for himself from the high school for recruiting me. He was fined twenty-thousand yuan and was also held responsible for picking up the designated fees for overstaying my visa, which was another ten-thousand yuan. I couldn't walk away unscathed, though, so I was fined two-thousand yuan. They gave me the paperwork for a temporary ten day visa and told me to leave the country as soon as possible.

I wasted no time obtaining my temporary visa. It was processed in two days. In the meantime, I called my mother. I told her everything that happened with the police and that, to sum it all up, I was broke and needed help. I couldn't afford the plane tickets to leave on my own, and international flight prices were climbing higher each day. Once again, they came to my rescue, shelling out over twenty-five hundred US dollars for the earliest flight back to the US. When I went to pick up my visa, one of the detectives met me. He handed me my passport and told me, "You're more than welcome to come back to Jinan. Just make sure you do it legally next time, okay?" And so, stuffing my pride back into my suitcases, I left China.

Chapter 4

I returned to China later that year, this time traveling on a shiny new internship visa handed over by a large and well-established English training school in Jinan. The internship invitation letter stated I would receive a small monthly stipend for groceries and be provided an apartment. In reality, that meant I was being paid under the table, and the school issued a monthly bribe on my behalf. Despite my previous scare, this didn't bother me. It was so commonplace, it was essentially an expectation. I taught there for two years, enrolling myself in the Shandong Teacher's University (ShanShi for short) for advanced Chinese language courses along the way. I was a full-time student and a full-time employee, which was illegal. Students weren't supposed to work, and workers could only attend university with special permission. Overall, I was busy but felt fulfilled. I learned to keep my head down and out of trouble. I followed all the laws, except for the ones I was already breaking (and the laws against skinny dipping, but even then, my friends and I only got caught once), making sure I gave myself at least a week's time before traveling to Hong Kong for a visa renewal every six months.

By 2014, I was in my third semester of Chinese language courses at ShanShi and had picked up another job for a small, yet well-organized and deeply connected English training school. I was one of only two

English teachers, the other hailing from Poland. The school's owner was shrewd with an uneven temper, but the manager of the school was a kind and generous woman. Lucky for us, the owner was hardly ever there. He was just in it for the business, while the manager had a passion for our students and their growth.

I spent most of my free time with my ShanShi friends, hanging around the foreign student dorms even though I had my own apartment elsewhere. I craved community and connection, and I had grown particularly close to a woman named Samm. She was from New York state and came to China in 2013 with her friend and classmate, Kelley. They shared a dorm room together, which provided the perfect place to crash in the hours between classes letting out and work in the evening. The training school was only ten minutes away by taxi or about an hour away by bus, factoring in the flow of evening traffic. Considering the overall size of the city, this was considered nearby.

Samm enamored me. She was fierce and fiery, yet still a bit shy and reserved. Her fashion sense was impeccable, and thanks to her time spent in the theater department, her makeup always looked professional. She had no trouble at all picking up Chinese, and it felt like she breezed through classes. Though I'm sure if you asked her, she'd recount the innumerable hours of studying and character practice she devoted each and every day to... when we weren't busy running around.

Samm and I were both overweight in China, which bonded us together more. Still, Samm was smaller than I was, and thanks to a recent medical procedure, was dropping pounds like they were freshly baked yams. I had been losing weight, too, and started wearing dresses for the first time since I was a little girl. Thanks to Samm, my personal appearance was constantly improving, and she helped me recover a confidence in myself that I hadn't felt since attending high school. Armed with this newfound fortitude, we would hit the bars and clubs every weekend, loosening up our inhibitions and flirting with cute strangers or occasionally with our mutual foreign friends. Most foreigners knew not to date within your own friends' group, though—it always got messy in the end.

For Samm's birthday, we decided to end the night at a club located in the sports stadium. It was a big place, complete with its own KTV (China's famous karaoke lounge chain) and a large, bouncing dance floor that shook when jumped on. The club was rather seedy, and it was an unspoken rule that if you got on that dance floor, you could expect to be constantly groped by random strangers. If you're into that, it can be a fun experience. But if you're not into that, it can be very frightening. We mostly stayed away from this club, unless we knew we would be dancing with a group that included foreign men. Tonight, however, while feeling rather sexual, we decided to be bold.

It was well after midnight by the time we got to the club. We'd spent the earlier part of the night celebrating first with dinner then a heavy assortment of drinks on the front steps of the ShanShi dorms. The club was packed full of people, and in our drunken state, we decided that hitting the dance floor was more important than ordering a drink. As soon as we stepped onto the dance floor, our bodies began to pulse up and down to the rhythm of the bouncing floor. The mass of people quickly separated us, but I could see Samm batting hands away from her body. We were on the dance floor for maybe ten minutes before the groping got to be too much for Samm. In honesty, it was too much for most people. I personally found it stimulating to grope back at whatever hand was groping at me, and I would later come to the realization that this hypersexuality I was experiencing was a prominent side effect of bipolar disorder.

I saw Samm pushing her way back towards the edge of the dance floor (the bouncy floor was roped off, separating the mass of dancing people from the tables and booths around it) and followed her. I remember pulling her out from behind the ropes and swatting away the last groping hand poking out through the throng of bodies. I had been dancing in a corner with a very handsome man who looked… different. He had thick, almost wavy hair, a strong brow, a prominent nose, and a jutting chin with a thick goatee. He was only a couple of inches taller than I was, and he was muscular. From his accent, I could tell he wasn't from the area, but he was clearly still Chinese. The strange man's English name was Jackie, like Jackie Chan, although he spoke no English. He eagerly followed me off the dance floor and caught up with Samm and I. Samm was ready to leave, but the stranger said he was there with a group of friends. He said they'd love to meet us. We told them that if they'd go outside with us for some fresh air, we'd be willing to chat for a bit.

The handsome-looking stranger and three of his friends followed Samm and I outside, lighting up cigarettes as the cool October air hit our faces. Jackie introduced us to his friend, "Little Fat," but neglected to tell us the names of the other two men. Jackie and Little Fat were best friends. Little Fat was exactly what his name described him as. He was short, perhaps not even five-foot, and very pudgy. He was excited to meet us and even more excited that we were fat like him, too. Jackie soon divulged that he and his friends were Hui, a Chinese ethnic minority from Western China that practiced Islam. The Hui trace their roots back to the dawning of the Silk Road, when merchants from the Middle East, primarily Iranian traders, would take up roots on the Qinghai-Tibetan Plateau and its bordering provinces. These merchants married local women and started their own families in China. The Hui are the descendants of these people, and it shows distinctly in their faces. Many Hui people I've met have the perfect middle ground between Chinese and Middle Eastern features, with darker skin that easily tans and eyes that are often a spectacular shade of deep honey hazel.

As followers of Islam, the Hui observe strict dietary laws. They don't drink and don't eat pork. Most will only eat from halal restaurants, while others will still eat chicken and beef that hasn't been blessed. Fish is free game for everyone, though, as it is considered inherently halal. The men frequently wear taqiyyas, and married women are expected to wear headscarves. Most Hui are Sunni, with the majority practicing Gedimu, China's earliest school of Islam. Jackie and his friends moved to Jinan for work, as their families had opened up several LanZhou Pulled Noodle shops, a special noodle soup made fresh by hand rather than machine, served in beef broth with scallions, turnips, and thin roast beef slices. Jackie was the best noodle-puller among them. This group, like the Saudis, largely abandoned their spiritual and dietary restrictions after leaving home. In Jinan, nobody knew or cared who they were, and there were no nosy neighbors to judge them. They smoked. They drank. They had premarital sex. They were the bad boys!

So, when Jackie asked for my WeChat information, I gladly handed it out. WeChat was China's latest and greatest social media craze, second only to QQ as a technology standard. With WeChat, you could chat with just one individual or make groups of over 100. I was a founding member of the Jinan *Laowai* (foreigner) group chat and was always handing my user ID over to new friends for easy contact. WeChat also allowed you to post photos and statuses as "moments" where friends could scroll through the feed and react. It also facilitated the exchange of money using QR codes, and one could purchase train and plane tickets through the app. It far exceeded the sophistication and user friendliness of our Western social media outlets. Immediately, Jackie began texting me. What was I doing in China? Was I born with my hair like that? When can we meet up again? How about we go drinking tomorrow?

I truly was a bar rat in China. As a university student, I had the responsibility of attending classes Monday through Friday. As an English teacher, I had the responsibility of teaching classes Wednesday through Sunday. This left me with no day to relax and let off steam—every morning required me to be somewhere by eight a.m. If I wanted to have fun, I would have to make my own. On Friday and Saturday nights, I would drink with my foreign friends who were there purely on business. They were an older crowd, in their early thirties to early sixties. On Sunday and Monday nights, I would drink with my English teacher friends who had Mondays and Tuesdays off. I was drinking four nights a week, not because I had a habit, but because I craved the social interactions that the bar and my wide array of friends had to offer. I felt like I was friends with at least one person from every little group of foreigners around Jinan, and I wanted to spend my time with all of them. My core friend group once even chastised me for trying too hard to integrate separate groups into one—they didn't always like each other. So, what was it if I added another group of friends to the mix? The next night, I went out drinking with Jackie.

Jackie was by far the coolest and most talented member of his group. He took me to a KTV to introduce me to more of his friends, again all men and all Hui. There were peanuts and pumpkin seeds strewn about the tables. The room was littered with bottles of pop and water. "We'll go drinking after this, because not everyone here right now likes to drink," he told me, then picked up the microphone to sing the next song. A *Hua'er* song came up on the screen, and he began belting out notes with perfect pitch. *Hua'er* is a genre of folk songs unique to the Northwest and Qinghai-Tibetan Plateau regions of China. These grassroots folk songs are sung by the Bao'an, DongXiang, Hui, Tibetan, Tu, and Yugu ethnic minorities. Often sung in duets, a large majority of *Hua'er* is about finding love and traditional romance. Hearing Jackie sing, my heart melted. Soon, one of his friends picked up the other microphone and joined in for the duet portion. His voice was like heaven, too!

"Can everyone here sing *Hua'er*?" I asked.

"No," said a man sitting next to me, fiddling with his taqiyya, "but we all like to listen."

I sang, too, not *Hua'er*, but a few of China's latest pop songs, a handful of traditional folk songs, and plenty of American jams from the 1990s and early 2000s. I consider myself to be a "good singer" so long as I can choose my octave. Jackie's group was in awe of my singing, offering calls of *"wa sai"* and clapping when I finished. Maybe I wasn't as good as Jackie, but I could carry a tune with little concentration.

I didn't say much to anyone aside from Jackie and Little Fat. I was feeling a little nervous. This was not because everyone was a man—

there are a lot of men in China—but because I was having a hard time understanding what everyone was saying. Everyone was speaking a different dialect of Chinese called *Qinghai Hua*, or Qinghai speech. I still wasn't used to the different dialect, and every region had its own.

Jinan had a gruff-sounding dialect called *Jinan Hua*, which my friend, Ken, could speak fluently. Ken had lived in China for close to a decade and was dead set on putting down roots in Jinan. He considered himself an immigrant in the country, although it would be a great hassle and even greater miracle if he could pin down official immigration paperwork. For non-Chinese citizens, immigrating to China is an absurdly complicated process. Ken tried to teach me *Jinan Hua*, but my tongue would always wrap around itself. The second and fourth tones were always switched, and the pronunciation of some words left my mouth feeling jumbled. *Qinghai Hua*, on the other hand, sounded like silk gliding through one's teeth punctuated with sporadic sharp K's and G's. Unfortunately, I never learned how to speak this dialect either, as I never had anyone who was willing to sit down and teach me. All of my Hui friends enjoyed having their own secret language. But who wouldn't?

Chapter 5

It didn't take long for Jackie and me to become an official couple. I spent several nights a week with Jackie and his friends, and the two of us would rent a hotel room in between his apartment and mine in order to get some alone time without leaving one or the other stranded too far away from home. Jackie lived with his uncle in the back of their noodle shop, and although I occasionally visited, it was all hands off while in front of his family. His elders were traditional in their faith and practices, and if they knew what Jackie was up to, they would forbid him from seeing his friends and I (even though he was a twenty-seven-year-old man). Along with his friends in Jinan, Jackie also introduced me to several online friends in QQ chat groups. They were Hui men and women who liked to sing, especially using a karaoke app called "ChangBa". We would record ourselves singing all sorts of songs, English and Chinese alike, and fight against our rival singing groups for who could get the most hearts and comments from other users.

Occasionally, Jackie would add me to a new group chat and introduce me as his foreign girlfriend. This brought him a lot of status, I realized. "Jackie managed to snag a foreigner! And she speaks Chinese! Wow! How did he pull that off?" Jackie wasn't a very attentive boyfriend, but he did like to show me off, and when we were actually together, he treated me like a precious butterfly. That is, until XiaXia got in the way.

I don't know exactly where XiaXia came from. She just showed up with the group one night, and everybody seemed to know who she was. She kept herself very close to Jackie, always sitting next to him, hanging on his arm, vying to sing duets with him. It bothered me, but she was obviously younger than I was, and Jackie didn't seem to be paying her much notice. So, I tried to keep my displeasure to myself. A couple of days later, XiaXia requested to be my friend on QQ. I accepted her request and began tearing through her profile. She had little information listed, but I gleaned that she was a worker for a local factory and lived in the on-site dorms that her factory provided. She shared a room with nine other women. Her profile showed photos from high school from two years prior and photo albums labeled with different cities that she'd visited.

"He's mine, you know," she messaged to me.

"Who?" I messaged back.

"Jackie. He likes me better than you, and he's going to be my boyfriend," she responded.

"I don't have time for this," I said. "You're practically still a child, and Jackie is almost thirty! Just leave him alone and find someone your own age."

"You'll see," she said, which concluded our conversation.

A week later, Jackie and I found ourselves in another hotel room. Just a dingy little hole in the wall, but all we wanted to do was hold each other, so we didn't need a lot of space. I was lying on his shoulders, fiddling with his goatee, when he asked me, "Do you love me?"

"What?" The question caught me off guard.

"Do you love me?" he repeated.

"I think maybe I do," I said. I couldn't determine whether my feelings constituted love or merely extreme infatuation.

"Then you should confess your love publicly. Anna, tomorrow in the group chat, declare your love for me in front of our singing team. I promise you won't be disappointed. Just trust me."

That night, I returned to my own apartment and thought a lot about what Jackie said to me. Why would he ask me that? I thought he was just having fun. I didn't think he was serious enough about me to fall in love with me! And what was he going to do after my confession? Would he confess back? Of course he would! Why else would he want me to do this? Maybe he wants a bit of a show… first the foreigner confesses her love for him, then he confesses his love for her, and it's a whirlwind of romance, just like in the movies we would watch. Okay, he'd won me over. I decided to go along with it. The next morning, I logged into WeChat and sent a message to the group: "Everyone, I have a confession to make… I'm in love with Jackie!"

He immediately responded, "Anna, my dear, you are so sweet. I know you are in love with me, but I cannot say that I love you, too! I'm in love with XiaXia!"

My heart sank to my stomach as hot tears welled up in my eyes. How could he say such a thing? I was not only confused by his declaration of love for XiaXia but more bewildered as to why he would goad me into confessing my love publicly, only to embarrass me. XiaXia wasn't even a part of this group, so she wouldn't see these messages unless he showed them to her… how long had they been conspiring to do this? Was this his idea or hers? Did Jackie really think so little of me? Then, one of the group members sent me a private message. It was Lilly, a Hui woman in her thirties who lived in Qinghai. She was married with children and had a deep and sultry singing voice. We duetted together on many occasions.

"What happened?" she asked, "I thought you and Jackie were really happy together?"

"I thought so, too," I said, "but I guess I was wrong. I didn't even know he was into XiaXia like that!"

"I don't like XiaXia," Lilly said. "She's too conniving."

"Do you know that much about her?" I asked. And it turned out Lilly knew quite a bit.

XiaXia was only sixteen years old. She dropped out of high school at the age of fourteen to become a worker instead of trying to pursue higher education. She'd made it through middle school, but her grades weren't good enough to even attempt to place well in the college entrance exams. This wasn't unusual in China. Many times, youth opted to join the workforce early to help pay family expenses, and teenagers living in rural areas would often give up their schooling in order to work the fields. The factories were like the working fields of the city. Furthermore, Jackie had been having sex with XiaXia for at least two weeks. How did Lilly know? XiaXia told her. I believed this information. The age of consent in China was only fourteen, so in the eyes of the men around her, she was fair game.

"But she's just a child! She's only sixteen! He's twenty-seven!" I typed furiously.

"I know. I don't think it's right, either," Lilly replied. "Men are dogs and don't really care about us. You'd be better off forgetting about Jackie. But don't worry, we will all still be your friends. I'm not the only one who feels this way."

That concluded my relationship with Jackie. I took it unexpectedly hard. I cried in class. I cried in the dorms. I wanted Jackie back, even though I was disgusted with him. Samm held me back from texting him. I couldn't understand why I was so obsessed with him, but I was. Maybe it was because he had rejected me so ruthlessly that made me want him. Don't we always want what we can't have? XiaXia wanted what she couldn't have, but she *did* have him. She stole him from me! No, I couldn't let myself think like that. XiaXia was just a child. The reasoning part of her brain wasn't fully developed yet. I didn't have to like her, but I shouldn't be sitting here blaming her. After all, Jackie was a man of his own free will. He made his own choices. He chose a child over me, and for that he could go burn. Oh, but I missed him. I shed tears for days.

My friends and my cats tried to make me forget about Jackie as much as they could. I had two cats in Jinan—an apple head Siamese cat named Phoebe and a white cat with orange blotches named Midas. I purchased Phoebe for 500 yuan at a pet store near my house. The pet store considered her a discount cat because of her kinked tail. The cramped conditions in her cage with her mother and siblings resulted in frequent fighting. Her crooked tail was a result. I purchased Midas from a street vendor near Daming Lake in the center of the city. He cost me 15 yuan and was handed to me in a plastic bag.

Even my new Hui friends checked in on me. It felt like an enormous scandal in the singing group, and I'm sure it felt like unnecessary drama for my foreign friends. My Chinese friends told me that I should forget about someone who spends all his time at bars and instead settle down with a nice Chinese man who didn't get into all that trouble. They glossed over the fact that I spent all of my time at bars, too. Being at the bar with my friends was exactly what helped me get over Jackie, along with a little nature therapy climbing Thousand Buddha Mountain and petting my feline friends.

They lived like kings in my apartment compared to how most pets in China were treated. Over the years, I'd asked many Chinese friends why pets were treated as objects rather than living things. The most common answers that I got were that animals do not have souls, animals do not have feelings, and animals are easily replaceable things that are not as important as humans. I distinctly remember one day when a third-grade student brought in a baby duck to show her classmates. During our break time, she and three other classmates took it outside to the parking lot, where they proceeded to toss it back and forth to each other at greater and greater distances until its neck snapped and it died. The child was disappointed, but not sad, and discarded the duckling in the trash bin before heading back to class. That being said, I have also met plenty of Chinese people who take exceptionally good care of their animals, even those who believe that their animals are like family. This was not the norm, however. At least not at that time in Jinan.

So compared to the other cats in the neighborhood, my cats made out like bandits on a daily basis. Their favorite activity was to jump up on the tile counter of the sunroom, where I hung my laundry to dry and tried to keep several plants alive, and bask in the warm sun that filtered in through the large, dirty windows. When the weather was pleasant, I would open the windows for them to enjoy the breeze. When I would cry, Phoebe would come comfort me. She was a highly intelligent cat and tuned in to human emotions. Midas couldn't really care one way or the other, but he was incredibly goofy and always got himself into impossible situations. Even though he never tried, he could always elicit a laugh from me. I am continually amazed at the scale of how a pet can make one feel better. My cats made life in China a little brighter, and I don't think I would have experienced as much joy from the world without them.

Chapter 6

About a week after Jackie and I broke up, I received a friend request from one of the members of the Hui singing group.

"He's married, you know," the text read.

"Who?" I responded.

"That Jackie guy, he's married," he replied.

"How do you know?" I asked.

"Just trust me, I know. I know him, and I can promise you that he has a wife and kid back home. He's just a playboy, and he's not worth your time," typed this mysterious stranger.

"Who are you?" I asked. "And how come you're in the group but never sing?"

"My name is Alimu," he replied, "and I just like to listen."

I wasn't put off by Alimu request to be friends. Everybody was friends in China. You could make a friend on the street, and they'd be a friend for life, expecting some *guanxi* (the mutual reciprocity of favors in terms of personal connections) at a later date, of course. Plus, I was no stranger to talking to random people. It happened every day—on the bus, on the street, in the restaurants, in the grocery stores—people just wanted to talk. They were curious. I was curious, too. Alimu and I texted each other for several hours that night. Most of it was the usual generic question. Where are you from? Why are you in China? How old are you? How did you get your hair like that? How did you meet Jackie? And now you have a bunch of Hui friends? The conversation was pleasant enough, but I wasn't really invested. I was more concerned about whether Jackie really was married with a family! In between the texts from Alimu, I would scour Jackie's social media accounts for clues. I found none. If Jackie was hiding anything, he was hiding it well, but this Alimu guy seemed so certain. Just trust him because he knows?

"How do you know for sure Jackie is married? Did he tell you?" I texted.

"No, he didn't tell me. But I know him, just trust me," Alimu texted back.

I let it be for the rest of the night and simply enjoyed my conversation with my new friend. He was polite, and a little funny, and he was trying his best to occupy my mind so I wouldn't feel so sad. He told me as much. When our conversation eventually came to a natural conclusion, I went to bed trying to digest the information I'd just been told.

The next morning, Alimu sent me another text message. "Good morning," it read. I texted "good morning" in response. There was silence until lunchtime when he texted me again, "Have you eaten?" This was a standard afternoon greeting in China. Asking if someone has eaten yet shows that you care about them and their health. I hadn't eaten yet, but I told him I had. I asked him if he'd eaten yet. He had. All was well. Later in the evening, he texted again, "What are you doing?" I was at home that night, not out on the town. A rarity for me. I told him as much and he told me not to worry, he'd be more than happy to entertain me with conversation. I was slow to respond to him and felt the intrusions to be a bit annoying. Still, I knew he was just trying to be nice, and he had obviously been thinking about me enough to ask me about my day three times. That was a pretty kind gesture, wasn't it? It felt nice to be thought of, but I was mentally drained. I didn't feel much like chatting with a stranger, but I didn't want to be completely alone either, so we texted lazily throughout the night.

The next few days, there was silence between us. He didn't text me, and I didn't text him. I didn't even notice, really. I thought him to be just another passing character in my life, here for one moment and gone for the next, but to my surprise, he popped up again one day.

"Hello, Anna! Have you eaten?" the screen read.

"Yes, I've eaten, thank you. And you?" I responded.

"Yes, yes, I've eaten! Thank you! What are you doing now?" he asked.

And our conversation picked up again. Throughout the course of the day, I asked Alimu the same questions that usually get thrown at me. I learned that he was Hui, his school name was Ma JunJie, and Alimu is the name that his Imam assigned him at birth. He was from northwestern Qinghai, in the Qilian Mountains. There, he herded yaks with his family. He was twenty-eight years old and had a brother, a sister, and a half-brother. Since his family was an ethnic minority, they could have as many children as they wanted. I also learned that his father died when he was ten, and holding to the local customs, his father's eldest brother married his mom to take care of the family in his father's absence. I learned that he loved the ocean, and he showed me a photograph of himself: baggy white t-shirt, cargo shorts, and long, floppy hair adorning his body that splashed through the waves with the biggest, goofiest smile I'd ever seen on any face. What a character!

But after that night, there was once again radio silence from Alimu. After the second day, I reached out to initiate the conversation. "What are you doing?" I texted, but there was no response. After the third day, I was disappointed that I didn't have an active talking buddy anymore but figured he'd come back eventually, and if not, at least we had a few good conversations. After the fourth day, a text came in!

"Did you miss me?" it read.

"Miss you? No, I didn't miss you," I replied, even though I actually had missed him a little.

"I'm in Jinan!" he wrote.

"What?! What are you doing in Jinan? Where are you?" I asked excitedly.

"I'm here on business. I had to sell a work truck. I drove it all the way out to Jinan, and now I have to fly back," he said.

"Can we meet up before you have to go? It'll be my treat!" I offered.

"No, I'm already at the airport, and I'm leaving soon," he replied.

How odd, I thought to myself, that he would come to Jinan and not even tell me until it was already too late. I told him as much, and he responded that he didn't say anything because he was too nervous, and he didn't believe that I'd want to meet up with him anyway. He was intimidated by the fact that I was a foreigner and didn't think I'd be able to make time for him in my busy schedule.

"Don't worry," he told me, "I'm in Jinan often. I'll be back again, and we can meet up then."

That sounded fine to me. If we were still talking by the time "next time" came around, we'd both be much more comfortable meeting up. Perhaps I could arrange a dinner with friends, both foreign and Chinese, and introduce him to our nightlife in Jinan. Did he drink? I didn't know. I hadn't asked, and I couldn't just assume that a Hui man didn't drink, considering all the avidly drinking Hui men that I'd come to know. Regardless, we could still have a fun time without drinking. There were plenty of group activities available to us at night, and we tried to diversify ourselves as much as possible.

Soon, hearing from Alimu became a daily occurrence. I began looking forward to his texts. We mostly had conversations about nothing, just endless small talk, but it was pleasant. It felt nice to have someone genuinely interested in my day. I was genuinely interested in his days, too, and he would send me photos of his yak herd, his campsite, the rolling mountains, and azure-blue skies of the Qinghai-Tibetan Plateau. He showed me photos of his family, and I came to learn that he had another younger half-sister still in high school. He must have told her about me, too, because it wasn't long before she requested to be my friend on QQ. I accepted, and she asked if I could help her with her English homework. I agreed. She then asked me for 50 yuan so she could go see a movie in the city with her friends. I declined that request, sending a screenshot of the conversation to Alimu. I didn't hear from her again.

In the meantime, I decided to question Jackie about his supposed family. We had been broken up for weeks, but were still members of the same karaoke team, and therefore still in a lot of the same social circles. I wasn't going to let a stupid breakup tear me away from this singing group I both enjoyed so much and performed so well in. Jackie could go kick rocks for all I cared, and I wavered between not caring at all and caring a hell of a lot. Jackie was still cordial to me and liked to pretend we were still friends. He would occasionally message me with a "have you eaten today?" to which I would always respond that I had and offer him the same pleasantries, but there was nothing of value left. Still, my curiosity got the better of me, and I decided to confront him about what Alimu told me.

"Alimu says you're married," I texted, "and he says he knows you."

"Who?" he replied, "I don't know anyone by that name."

I sent him Alimu's picture.

"No, I don't know him. He doesn't know me," Jackie insisted.

"But are you married?" I pressured.

"I used to be," he said, "but we divorced two years ago. I don't like to talk about it."

"What about kids?" I asked.

"I have a son," he said and sent me a photo of a seven-year-old boy with a closely shaved head who looked just like his father. It hurt a little knowing that he had a son that he never told me about. It felt like further confirmation that he was never serious about me and that I was just his temporary plaything. He had already broken up with XiaXia, and it soon became clear to me that Jackie truly was the embodiment of a stereotypical Chinese playboy, and he was proud of it. Alimu gloated when I told him about my conversation with Jackie.

"I told you!" he typed, "I told you he had a family and you didn't believe me. Look, now you have no reason not to believe me. Please trust me. I'm only trying to do right by you." And that was the last moment I spent pining over Jackie.

Chapter 7

My friendship with Alimu blossomed, and conversations with this once-mysterious internet stranger became an expectation. We shared our days and lives with each other, and I spent my free time between dinner and bedtime, and sometimes even a little after bedtime, texting Alimu. One night, he asked if he could call me. He said wanted to know what my voice sounded like, to put a sound to a face. He was also curious to know if I could actually speak Chinese as well as I could type it, so I obliged him, and my phone soon rang.

His voice was of medium range, a strong tenor with a sense of whimsy in the throat. He spoke softly, yet his voice carried a strong air. "Can you understand what I'm saying?" he asked.

"Of course I can," I giggled.

And that was just about all I could understand. His accent was strong, and his word choice was full of phrases I didn't know, words I'd never heard of, or *chengyu* (four-character idioms) with which I was unfamiliar. He then switched to *Qinghai Hua* for a bit of amusement. I couldn't understand that either, but Alimu was patient with me. Despite me asking *shenme* (what) after every sentence he spoke, he slowed and repeated himself until I could understand the conversation. We talked for two hours that night, until the minutes on my phone ran out.

At that time in China, all cell phones were networked through one of four major networks. You could buy a SIM card and new phone number from any of the numerous cell phone stands around the city, with at least one of the two biggest companies present in almost every neighborhood. You could even find prepaid SIM cards carried by some cigarette and snack vendors, setting up shop with their carts along side streets and alleyways. It cost roughly 100 yuan for 1G of data, and that was split between voice, text, and internet usage. I rarely used my phone to call people and could generally get away with only topping up my phone payments once every two weeks, depending on how often I used my data—and I used a lot of data. Still, this was the first time a phone conversation had run me out of funds for my account.

The next night, we talked again for two hours. This time, it was easier for me to understand him, but at least every other sentence was still punctuated by my *shenme?* in response. His phone ran out of minutes this night, and I felt bad that I'd made him use up so much of his data just to talk to me. Rural yak herders in China don't make much money. The rural population in general didn't make much money. For some, that meant waiting until the end of the month to top up your phone's data again. I didn't want him to be without, especially on my behalf, and truthfully, I wanted the chance to at least say goodnight instead of just abruptly ending the conversation when the phones disconnected. It was growing late, though, and the closest shop with a China Mobile kiosk set up closed at 10pm. I rushed out of my apartment and mounted my bike. I had ten minutes to get to the shop before closing.

I scooted in the doorway just before the store closed. The shopkeeper greeted me warmly. He was a friend, and I stopped in his shop almost every day for a soft drink and a pack of smokes, or occasionally some jarred longans in syrup and five-spiced beef jerky.

"Anna! Good to see you! Would you care to stay for a drink?" he asked as he held up a bottle of Qingdao beer.

"Not tonight, my friend, I've got an early day tomorrow," I replied.

"Didn't you just put money on your phone yesterday? And you've already used all your data?" he inquired.

"This time it's for a friend," I said, and wrote down Alimu's number for the shopkeeper to enter into his system.

"You're a good friend, then," he said, and smiled at me.

Standing outside the shop, I tried to call Alimu back. It rang, which meant the data payment had processed, but there was no answer. I mounted my bike again and rode back home. Once upstairs, I called again. This time he answered.

"I put some money on your phone!" I exclaimed, "I didn't want you to have to spend all that money just for me." For many people in China, spending 100 yuan was a luxury. For many foreign teachers living in Jinan, spending 100 yuan was an almost-daily occurrence. I personally spent money very easily. Payday always came with a special trip to the mall for foreign cheese and delicacies, which ate up close to 1,000 yuan per visit. I rarely cooked at home, and I generally opted for taxis for transportation instead of public buses. In China, the overabundance of taxis and cheap cab fare made it feel like another form of public transportation in and of itself, so spending 100 yuan to make a friend's life a little easier was nothing. To be honest, I wasn't good with my money in China. I didn't have any savings—I spent everything I earned—but I lived an exquisitely privileged life while there.

Alimu thanked me for going out of my way for him. Otherwise, it would have been a week before he could top up his data. He still had Wi-Fi access, so would be able to chat on QQ and WeChat when he was home at nights, but if it weren't for my generosity, he wouldn't be able to use his phone out on the mountains. Not that he had much service in the mountains to begin with. Being so far away, the infrastructure to provide data to the Qinghai-Tibetan Plateau's farthest reaches was just in its infancy. Sometimes you could take five steps to the left and get a signal. Take five more steps, and the signal is gone. Still the signal was strong in town, and I could tell where he was in his daily schedule by the frequency at which I received his texts.

We wished each other a good night, and I slipped off to sleep with Alimu on my mind. My friends had started noticing, too. His name was on my lips often, but Samm wasn't a fan of him. She told me it was too soon after Jackie to start getting obsessed with anyone, and maybe I should just slow down. Besides, wasn't it bothering Alan that I was talking on the phone for literal hours on end in our shared living room?

Alan was my ex-boyfriend. He was from rural Inner Mongolia, in an extremely small village that farmed sunflowers and poplar trees. Alan was a great guy and a loyal friend, but his ultimate life goal was to move back to Inner Mongolia and be close to his parents. I did not share his dream; it was too lifeless in his village, and while I usually didn't mind being cooped up some place with nothing to do, I needed some spice in life, a little adventure, a dollop of uniqueness to dip my finger into every now and then. That just wasn't something Alan could provide. Luckily, our breakup was amicable, and we continued to share an apartment together for some time.

Alan started living with me early in our relationship. We worked for the same English training school—him in the marketing department—but his income was less than a quarter of mine. I was astounded when I first saw the apartment where he lived. It was located down a decrepit alley on the northern side of the city. He shared the apartment with five other men in only three rooms. There was no heating and no air conditioning. The walls were bare concrete, the windows didn't fit into their panes, and the chipping ceiling paint would flutter down like snowflakes. He had no privacy and hated where he lived, but this was the life of a young rural bachelor. What could he do? I made the offer for him to join me in my apartment not long after visiting his apartment. He was eager to say yes, paid a small portion of the rent (slightly more than what he was already paying) and helped keep the place tidy.

When we split, Alan moved out of my bedroom and into the spare. It was hard to find affordable living arrangements, and I couldn't just kick him out on the street. The lease was in my name, but this was a person who, despite being an absolute ass immediately after our breakup, had joined me on a year of adventures. I even introduced him to my father when he came to visit China. I had no ill will against Alan, but my horse was also no longer hitched to that wagon. In fact, my horse had been galloping alone for miles. Alan didn't seem to mind my phone conversations with Alimu. We didn't see much of each other, and he usually locked himself away in his room with a cat or two after dinner. Still, he was wary of Alimu in general. He told me to be careful about who I was talking to and that not everybody who seems nice *is* nice, especially in China. Samm felt the same way initially, although I convinced her that Alimu was not, in fact, one of the not-so-nice guys. She eventually conceded and began inquiring about Alimu daily.

Chapter 8

I gladly talked about Alimu. I had such a crush on him! From the pictures he'd shown me, he was deviously handsome with hair that hung down into his eyes. He was always in jeans and a leather jacket, knew how to ride horses, and was close to his family. He consistently made me laugh and seemed to always make space for me in his days, despite being tired from long hours shepherding on the mountain. We talked on the phone most nights now, sometimes just a few minutes and sometimes for hours. It seemed like we never ran out of things to talk about, and by now I had no problems understanding what he was saying, aside from the occasional odd character that I would have to translate. He had learned to talk to me, and I had learned to talk to him. Communication will always find a way. Unlike Jackie, Alimu wasn't really interested in showing off his new foreign friend. He told his siblings about me, but he didn't flaunt our friendship in the group chats like Jackie had done before. I found this to be a relief. Not everybody had to know our business, and I was tired of feeling like a novelty toy.

It was February now, and the Spring Festival was drawing near. This meant everyone would have a two-week break from work and school so people could travel home and be with their loved ones for the new year. Samm was away for a couple of days, and she let me use her apartment as an escape from my own. I had run into some trouble with my internet provider, and it meant being without for two weeks. Unfortunately, that didn't mesh with my plans to keep up with prime-time American television. I wanted to watch dragons and see ice zombies and gore! After sponging off Samm's internet for an episode or two, I called Alimu.

That night, he sent me a picture that included his hand, and I noticed that he was missing his left pinky finger! Not all of it, just the tip, but enough to be noticeable. I decided to bring it up.

"What happened to your finger, Alimu?" I asked. "It looks like it got cut off!"

"It did," he replied. "And I'm the one that did it."

And so, he told me the story of how he lost his pinky. Years ago, he was in love and engaged to be married. Unfortunately, the relationship with his fiancée had been deteriorating, and she soon became suspicious and jealous of him. She kept accusing him of sleeping around with other women. She decided to leave him. He begged her not to, told her that he would do anything to make her stay. He loved her! They were meant for each other! Please, wasn't there anything he could do? As it turns out, there was one demand she had in mind: cut off his pinky to prove that he loved her. After all, what's a pinky compared to love? Surely, he could sacrifice just a tiny part of himself on her behalf. So, he took a meat cleaver from the kitchen, placed his hand on a carving block, and chopped off the tip of his pinky. He told me it bled like hell but didn't really hurt until after he got to the hospital. His fiancée left him anyway, claiming that he was too crazy to be with. Anyone who would be willing to mutilate themselves for a lover must be crazy, right?

I found the story rather romantic. Perhaps I could see myself in his position. If the person I truly loved and wanted to marry was walking out of my life, I could see myself meeting their demands for a pinky. I might make my significant other chop it off, though, as I faint when encountering blood. When I later told the story to Samm, she physically recoiled. It was too much, she said. Chopping off a pinky was taking it too far. I agreed with her that the whole ordeal was overkill, but this happened when Alimu was much younger, in his early twenties. He'd had almost a decade of time to grow and heal himself emotionally since then, so why not give him the benefit of the doubt? I couldn't imagine anyone cutting off more than one small finger, perhaps a toe?

And bringing up the topic of a fiancée led me to my next question. Was he married? It wouldn't have been the first time a married man had caught my eye, but I didn't go after married men. Although unfortunately, at that time in China, having a mistress was not always a deal breaker in a marriage. In fact, some women just assumed their husbands would cheat, citing that men can't control themselves, and as long as they're still bringing home the bacon and treating the kids right, so what if he has a little honey with his tea on the side? Alimu has previously told me that Hui men and women generally marry as soon as they're adults, with families putting pressure on youths as young as sixteen to settle down. Most marriages were arranged, and children were expected right away. You grow up, you get married, and you start a family. The family that you make takes care of the elderly, and eventually you, as the years pass by.

But didn't this mean that Alimu should be married by now, too? Wouldn't his family have pressured him into an arranged marriage by now? He assured me that he was, in fact, single. Never married, no kids. It just didn't happen for him. After his fiancée left him, he decided not to pursue love anymore, it just wasn't worth the pain. I could understand that perspective. Imagine mutilating yourself for your lover, only to have them leave. That would be hard for anyone to fully recover from and would certainly leave me jaded about future relationships. I had no reason not to take Alimu for his word. After all, he was spending hours every night chatting with me in some way or another. Would he be able to spend entire evenings on the phone with me if he had a wife and family? Of course not, that would be absurd! I felt a little silly for questioning his relationship status, given the amount of attention he paid to me every day. We weren't dating, though. Not officially a couple. It might be nice to be, though, wouldn't it? Even though he was literally a thousand miles away, he had become the highlight of my days. I couldn't talk about him without smiling. I couldn't think about him without smiling.

I felt like a schoolgirl with my belly full of butterflies, but I took a leap of faith. Squinting my eyes tight and holding onto my cell phone for dear life, I asked him, "What do you think if *we* were a couple?"

"Are you asking me to be your boyfriend?" he asked, then immediately responded, "I can be your boyfriend, if you want me." Of course I wanted him. I told him as much, and we made it official: we were a couple.

I left Samm's that night with a spring in my step. Even Alan noticed it, although he rolled his eyes when I told him about my new relationship status.

"Just be careful," he urged. "You can't always trust people like *him*."

I wasn't quite sure what Alan was referring to when he said "people like him," but it wasn't uncommon for Chinese people to make generalized stereotypes about others from certain provinces. In fact, I remember Zhen constantly being teased for being from Henan, which was famous for its "crafty tricksters" and "clever thieves". Anyone from Henan will try to trick you out of your money, I often heard people say. So maybe there was a bit of disdain for Alimu because he was from Qinghai province, where the people are known as "tigers". Surely there wasn't discrimination against his economic status, given that Alan was from the same social class as Alimu, or perhaps it was the fact that he was Hui and Muslim that threw Alan off and made him so uneasy. The local people in Jinan didn't always have favorable views of Muslims, with some exclaiming that they are all terrorists and that their religion should be banned from China. This negative view of Muslims truly surprised me, as Jinan was famous for its Muslim Quarter barbeque, for which folks would travel from distant cities away to try.

To be honest, I wasn't sure how dedicated to his religion Alimu was. I knew he kept halal, but I also knew he'd drunk alcohol in the past. He attended mosque, but I was unaware of how often. Also, I knew he wasn't opposed to premarital sex because of his past fiancée (I asked). I deduced that he wasn't as hardcore about his faith as others but wasn't as casual about it as Jackie and his friends, either. That was fine with me. At the time, I was still a practicing Pagan, although my ideals pulled from multiple religious thoughts. I could be with a Muslim man. I could be with a Chinese Muslim yak herder from the Third Pole of the World, and I would not let anybody scoff at me for that. I was excited about the possibilities. Maybe I could even be a yak herder myself! Now that would be the life, spending the warm seasons herding yaks around the hillsides and spending the winter months teaching or writing or something substantial to earn money during the cold. I admit, I let myself get a little carried away with the fantasies. I was looking for something unique, and that's exactly what I got.

But Alimu started to pull away from me immediately after declaring us a couple. I wasn't sure what had changed, but his messages became less frequent throughout the day, and suddenly he didn't have time for phone calls at night. He told me he was just busy and not to worry about it, just give him a little bit of space for a little bit of time. It was hard to resist reaching out to him, but I understood that being busy could be stressful for some and not everyone was as attached to their phones all day like I was. Eventually Alimu came back, about a week later, and although our constant texting had slowed down, he still called every night. One night, he brought up the idea of visiting him for Spring Festival.

"How would you like to come see me?" he asked.

"I'd love to," I said, "but I don't have any way to get there!"

"Don't worry, I know a guy at the airport who can get you some plane tickets. Just hold on for a day or two," he said. "Then you can visit my whole family for the break! We don't celebrate the Spring Festival, but it would still be a convenient time for you to come."

I was elated! I would get to visit Alimu! On top of that, I'd finally get to see this Qinghai all of my Hui friends spoke so poetically about, and I'd get to see a yak! I'd never seen a yak in real life before. So, we set a date for the visit. Alimu told me when I arrived, he'd meet me at the airport. Then we'd first travel to Xining, the capital city, where we'd catch a long-distance bus for the six-hour journey to Qilian and then another two-hour bus ride to his hometown. When I told my friends about Alimu's offer to buy me a plane ticket to visit him, I received mixed replies. Some friends were happy for me, saying how generous Alimu was and how this was the perfect opportunity to go chase love. Who knows where the road might lead? Others were more practical. What if he's just trying to lure you out there? Do you really know anything about him? What if he kidnaps you for ransom and we have to go save your overly-optimistic ass?

Their concerns were not lost on me. In fact, I didn't really have any proof that Alimu was he who said he was. We had never had a video chat, which was fine by me. I didn't like video conversations, and his internet connection was never stable enough to transmit a live video. Sure, I'd seen his pictures and heard his voice, but I also knew how catfishing worked and didn't want to wind up in a dangerous situation. I needed some reassurance. When I told this to Alimu, he was completely understanding. Immediately, he sent me a photo of his driver's license. The license had the name *Ma Nai* written in the name field.

I asked him about this, wasn't his name Alimu? He explained that he had many names. There was the name he was born with that his mother and father gave him, which was Ma Nai, but the nurse had typed in the wrong character for his last name on his birth certificate, and instead of the character *ma* that represents the common last name of "horse", he was given the character *ma* that represents the word for "hemp" or "coarse and pitted", depending on its context. He also had the name that his Imam gave him shortly after his birth, which was Alimu. This is what his family called him. Then he had his school name, which was a standardized common-tongue name given to school children with non-traditional names to help them properly integrate. That name was Ma JunJie, which is what his classmates and teachers called him. It all seemed quite complex, but a quick ask of a fellow Hui friend confirmed that this was very commonplace, everything from the wrong character in the name to being called something else entirely at school. "All right," I thought to myself, "so that checks out."

The license also displayed his personal identification number—similar to a social security number, except used more widely. If you want to buy a train ticket, you need your number. If you want a job, you need your number. If you want to buy a house, you need your number. If you want insurance or to open a bank account or sometimes to buy from online stores, you need your number. I typed his number into the Baidu search engine, wondering if anything would pop up. Arrest records? Did they even keep those in China? But nothing indicated a red flag in the search, and if I had his number, then I could give it to a friend in case I needed the police, and they would know exactly who to look for and where to look for him. All personal numbers corresponded to the county where the individual was born, the birthdate of the holder, and a series of numbers at the end to differentiate between multiple people with the same location and birthdate. Having access to this number was pretty serious stuff.

Of course, his license also listed his address. It was listed as YangLong Village, HaiBei County, Qinghai Province. I immediately found a satellite map online and pinpointed exactly where this village was. It was absolutely in the middle of nowhere, eight hours from the nearest city, but surrounded by beautifully sloping mountains and steppe. After a bit more research, I made a startling discovery. The entirety of HaiBei county was off-limits to foreigners! With a secret military base sitting deep withing the Qilian mountains, the government closed off the area to outsiders. Still, I found plenty of personal accounts and social media pages that showcased foreigners visiting Qilian and the mountains. One recounted his story of being caught in the county. He was stopped after three days and asked to leave by the local police. They escorted him to the nearest bus station and watched him buy a ticket before sending him on his way. I decided that wasn't so bad. If I was caught, I would simply be asked to leave, and of course I would comply. Still, who would even know I was there? The experience was worth the risk. I had a photo with his name, ID number, address, and picture, all in one neat little package. I sent this photo to Samm and Alan to keep safe in case anything went wrong, and after deciding that I was satisfied enough with the information I had, I waited for the plane tickets.

Except the tickets never came. Each day, Alimu told me to keep waiting. He was sure his friend would come through. He's just working out some kinks. But our selected travel date was rapidly approaching, and I was getting anxious. Finally, the night before arrived, but I was still ticketless, and even worse, I couldn't get ahold of Alimu! My phone calls were all bouncing back due to lack of service, and he wasn't online to chat with, either. He must be somewhere without service, I thought. Maybe he's traveling to meet me, considering it was such a long trip. Did that mean he would be expecting me at the airport? What should I do? After a fair share of pacing and hand-wringing, I made the decision to purchase my own tickets, spending nearly two thousand yuan on the last-minute purchase during the entire year's peak travel time.

I now believe, looking back, this was part of a hypomanic episode. My bipolar disorder had a strong presence in China, and I can now identify which parts of my life were most likely affected by my drastic changes in brain chemistry. I don't know how much of my decision was fueled by logic and how much was fueled by a grandiose imagination of a movie-worthy romantic scene, where Alimu and I would run into each other's arms at the airport, our lips embracing in what would be the first of many long, passionate kisses. I couldn't lose the opportunity to have that moment, and if the world wasn't going to cooperate by giving me free plane tickets, I'd just have to pay for my own damned tickets and carve my own way.

Chapter 9

I woke up at five a.m. to catch my eight-fifteen a.m. flight out of Jinan. It was way too early for most of the breakfast vendors to be out, but I knew a guy who sold shredded stewed pork meat sandwiches every morning before dawn. They came topped with fresh tiger skin peppers and a hard-boiled tea egg. He set up his cart right outside my apartment building, just across the street in an alleyway next to the busy intersection. Grateful for his presence, I scarfed down the sandwich before hailing a taxi to the airport. It was about an hour's drive if the traffic behaved. We agreed upon a flat rate of a hundred yuan for the trip. This was done as a courtesy to the drivers. This early in the morning, the trip total should cost less than a hundred yuan, but going there this early also meant that the taxi driver would have to wait for a long time before the first plane arrived and he could pick up another customer. The extra money was to compensate for his waiting time. I shared a cigarette or two with the driver along the way. The vast majority of taxi drivers either smoked right along with their passengers or otherwise allowed passengers to smoke in their cars. In fact, it was rare to find a taxi who wouldn't let you smoke.

After arriving at the airport and getting through security, I pulled out my phone again. Still nothing from Alimu, but I wasn't too surprised, considering he was probably just getting up for breakfast. I sent him a message: "I bought my own tickets and I'm boarding the plane soon. I'll be there around one p.m. Let me know when you see this message!" Then I boarded the plane. I had a first-class seat, since those were the only tickets left. Immediately upon boarding, I was served a moist hand towel and a steaming glass of hot orange juice. Most breakfast juices were served warm. We touched down to transfer in Lanzhou. The next flight was packed full of men in patterned taqiyyas and women in elaborate and ornate head scarves. I could hear *Qinghai Hua, Gansu Hua,* and Tibetan on the plane. We were served a snack labeled in Chinese as halal, and I learned the plane had no alcohol. This felt like stepping into a whole new world. It certainly wasn't like the China I'd come to know.

The Xining airport was small but open. I gathered my bags then headed for the exit, hoping Alimu would be there, but I still hadn't received a reply. There were no text messages, he wasn't online, and he wasn't answering the phone. The phone was within service range now; he just wasn't picking up. I walked past the exit gates of the airport lobby and looked around. People spilled in and out of the doors, hurrying along to their final destinations, but none of these faces were familiar to me. Alimu wasn't there. What should I do now? I began to feel like a fool… I should have known that he was flaking out on me when he didn't pull through with the tickets, and now he's been ignoring me all day! He's too scared to show up, probably because he's a fake, right? I was so disappointed in myself.

But then again, maybe I was wrong to think so poorly of Alimu. What if he was hurt? What if he had already checked into a hotel room and was just on his way to get me? What if he was going to show up at any moment? I found a metal bench and waited. After sitting in the airport for two hours, a police officer noticed me. I told him I was waiting for my boyfriend to show up, but I'd never met him before, and now I couldn't get ahold of him. The officer asked if I had any more information about him, and I pulled out the photo of Alimu's license. The officer beckoned me to follow him into his office, where I watched him run Alimu's identification number through a database. He hadn't been arrested, and he wasn't on any blacklists. There was no criminal history, so I could rest easy that he wasn't an *outward* criminal, at least. Eventually, the officer lost interest in me and wished me a good day while he went back to patrolling the lobby.

I decided to text Jackie. I told him that I was in Xining, his hometown, and the person who was supposed to meet me never showed up. I asked him if he knew of any hotels that were on the cheaper side but were also allowed to take foreigners. Not every hotel in China has the proper paperwork and permissions to house foreign guests. He asked me to tell him the exact details of everything that happened, so I did. When I was finished, he responded with, "hang on, I'll call you in a few minutes." I waited half an hour for Jackie's call, but when I answered, he gave me the address of a hotel in a nearby city. It wasn't in Xining proper but a little to the east of the city. It was closer to the airport, and he had a cousin who owned the place. It wasn't too expensive, and they would take me in for a discount since I was Jackie's friend. This was a perfect demonstration of *guanxi*. When I asked him about permissions for foreigners, he responded with, "just don't ask." Fair enough, I thought. I was grateful for his help.

The hotel was quaint but clean. The bathroom was spacious, and the toilet was separated from the shower, a luxury not all Chinese bathrooms have. The bed wasn't too firm, and the pillows were soft enough to melt into. As I threw myself onto the bed, I heard my stomach gurgle. I was starving, and it was growing late. I managed to find a convenience store a few blocks away and picked up a couple bowls of instant noodles and several bottles of various juices and good things to drink. I was bummed about how the trip was turning out, and my heart was painfully aching for Alimu. I knew deep down there was always a possibility of getting duped, but I didn't want to think it was true. My return flight wasn't for several more days, so I began looking for ways to either change my flight to an earlier date or get a new flight out altogether. I didn't want to spend any more time than I had to just cooped up in a hotel with no place to go, and I wasn't in the mood to go exploring alone. But then, in the middle of it all, a chat window appeared. It was Alimu!

"I'm so sorry, Anna, I didn't think you'd actually come!" he wrote.

"Of course I came," I responded. "That was our plan!"

"I know, I'm sorry. I'm on my way to you now. Where are you?" he texted.

I sent him the address for where I was.

"Okay," he replied, "I'll be there soon. But it will be a few hours. Something bad has come up that I'm dealing with now. I promise, though, I'm doing everything I can to be with you."

"What's going on?" I typed frantically. "Is everything okay?!"

"No, but I can't explain it right now," he replied, "but soon. Just wait for me, I have to go now."

And then he was gone. Offline again. But at least he'd shown up! Maybe he wasn't physically here yet, but he was on his way. He said something bad had happened. What could it be? Was he in trouble? Was he hurt? There was nothing I could do but wait. And wait. And wait. It was driving me crazy. The hotel didn't have a TV in the room, so I took a walk. By now it was dark, and most businesses had closed. I found a few street food vendors, but nothing looked appetizing. I returned to my hotel room without making any new discoveries and without any food save for my instant noodles. Luckily, I knew of a way to pass the time. I called Samm.

I told her how the entire day had gone. She was flabbergasted, but excited that he was coming after all. She told me to stay positive, focus on the fact that he was trying to get to me, and in the meantime, she would be there to talk me through the waiting process. I was thankful for her presence, at least emotionally if not physically. I updated a few other friends, figured out the Wi-Fi password, and tried to occupy my mind with various tv shows on my laptop. Nothing worked, though. I couldn't keep my mind off Alimu. It was nearing 11pm when I heard from him again.

"Anna, have you eaten?" his text message read.

"A little," I replied. "Just some instant noodles. Have you eaten?"

"No," he said, "and I'm not going to make it there tonight, either. Things have gotten... complicated. I'll be there tomorrow, okay? I promise."

"Alimu," I typed, "please tell me what's going on. I've come all this way for you, and now I'm all alone. The least you can do is let me know why you've been delayed."

"Fine, but you can't tell anyone else! Not even your friends!" he responded.

The story went like this: He was riding with a group of friends in a car headed towards Xining. They were carpooling for the trek between YangLong and the province capital, but on the way, the driver hit a bear! And not just any bear, a sun bear. These are considered a protected species, and the bear was dead! He said they didn't expect it to come onto the road, but it ran right across the steppe and onto the highway where it collided with the car and died. They knew they were in trouble. Killing one of these bears could mean life in prison! So, they all agreed: instead of calling the police, they would take the bear somewhere and bury it. Then they would repair the car and never speak of it again.

Alimu told me that they put the bear in the trunk and drove to a friend of a friend's house who had a large amount of property with few neighbors. They buried the bear in his backyard, then drove the car to another friend's house to store for a few days before taking it to be repaired. Alimu was paranoid that the police were after him. Cameras were all over China's highways, and rural provinces were no exception. He was also worried that someone would dig up the bear to sell its body and organs on the black market, and if that happened, everybody ran the risk of being caught and prosecuted even further. For now, he was hunkering down at the friend of a friend's house, exhausted from digging a big hole all night.

I almost didn't believe his story. A bear? Yeah, right. But then he sent me a photo, and sure enough, there was a dead ring-neck bear on the side of the road, next to a car with a Chinese license plate. That was enough to keep me convinced. But what a story! I couldn't say I agreed with their course of action in burying the bear, but I understood the thought process. You really didn't want to be caught breaking laws in China, and I had no idea how severe the laws were regarding killing endangered species. Despite Alimu begging me otherwise, I told my friends the story. None of my friends believed him, but nobody could refute the photo evidence. Still, there were no people in the photo—just the bear and the car. Maybe he pulled the photo from online? But that would be such an elaborate ruse! Why make up a whole story about accidentally killing a bear and going on a mission to bury it instead of just saying something like, "sorry, my car broke down," or even, "I'm just not that into you and was busy doing not-you things."

I was feeling a little powerless in the situation. What were my options? I could accept the bear story and wait until tomorrow for Alimu to come or reject the bear story and tell Alimu to get lost while I left for home. The latter sounded like the least pleasant option. After all, I had come all this way. I'd flown literally across the entirety of China just to meet this man. I decided to finish what I had started and wait to see if Alimu would actually arrive. I tossed and turned in bed that night and spent a fair amount of time pouring through his social media again, looking for hints or clues that would give me any insight into what exactly Alimu was made of. Although these were photos and posts that I had seen a dozen times before, I couldn't help but wonder if there was something I had missed. However, I found nothing new and eventually gave in to a dreamless sleep.

I woke late the next morning, hungrier than a dead bear. No word from Alimu. I decided to go outside and try to find something to eat. Much to my disappointment, I found the surrounding streets full of textile and machine part businesses, two convenience stores, and not much else. There were no restaurants and no street food vendors, and I wasn't in the mood to venture out too far, in case Alimu were to arrive while I was gone. I grabbed a few items from one of the convenience stores and headed back inside. It was a meager brunch, but enough to keep my stomach from getting angry. At noon, I received my first message from Alimu.

It was a simple text of "I'm on my way, keep waiting" and was accompanied by a video. In the video, Alimu was riding a long-distance bus. He was dressed all in black, with a black face mask covering his nose and mouth. In China, it was common to see people wearing face masks any day of the week, especially if one was feeling ill or sought the warmth a mask would provide. Since Xining was cold enough to snow, he didn't look out of place in the slightest. Still, I could tell he was trying to hide his face from those around him. He sat low in the bus seat, hunkered up against the window. The video was short, maybe five seconds long, but it was enough to give both proof of life and proof that he was on his way. I didn't know where he was coming from, though, and was unsure how long the bus ride would take. I asked him.

"I don't know," he replied. "The bus has to go pretty slow because of the snow. We already had to help dig it out of a snowbank once. Just keep persisting."

The latter was a common phrase used to encourage the listener to keep enduring whatever hardship they were going through, to grit one's teeth and persist until the end. The snow in the city was barely falling, but the mountains didn't follow the same rules as the city. I would later see firsthand how the roads zigzagged above and below the mountains' snow lines, vehicles prisoner to the switchback roads that were littered with gravel at the peaks for better traction. But I hated waiting! And not knowing when he would arrive was driving me insane. I couldn't concentrate on anything.

After hours of waiting and worrying, I finally received the text I'd been waiting for: "I'm here." I quickly slipped my shoes on, straightened my outfit, and headed out to meet him. He wasn't in the hotel lobby. Maybe outside? He wasn't outside either. Until he was! As soon as he turned around, I knew it was him, and I ran up to him with my arms out wide for an embrace.

"Not here," he said firmly, and grabbed my arm. "Wait until we're inside."

I was taken aback. No hug? I felt so embarrassed for being rejected like that, but I tried to brush it off and led him inside to my hotel room.

We stepped in, and Alimu took a slow look around before sitting on the bed. He took off his shoes and face mask, breathed a sigh of relief, then stared at me.

"Come sit on my lap," he smiled and patted the tops of his thighs. They were thick thighs that filled out his pants, unlike most of the Chinese men I'd known, whose thighs were lean and slender. He wanted me to sit on his lap? I stared at him for a minute, not sure what to do.

"Are you afraid you'll crush me?" he laughed. "C'mon, you can't hurt me, I'm strong." This struck a bit of a chord with me. I'd been told those same words numerous times by other Chinese men. I was heavier than most people, even in America, and Alimu was shorter than I was. Of course, I knew I wouldn't crush him, but he might not anticipate just how heavy I was, and that would lead to a truly awkward moment. I didn't want to reject him either, especially while he had the biggest smile on his face. He beckoned me over again, and so I went. I sat gingerly in his lap, trying not to put my full weight on his legs. "No," he said, "just sit!" And he wrapped his arms around me and held me tight against his body. Then he gently placed a hand on my face and pulled me towards him, kissing me deeply and with desire.

Our first kiss! Sparks spiraled around my brain and body. I'd thought this moment would never come, and was rather pleased to find he was quite a good kisser. It felt so natural, with his hands on my body and my body pressed against his. I could feel his warmth even through his jacket. It wasn't long before we replaced our clothes with bed sheets and got to know one another on a deeply personal level. We explored each other's bodies for what seemed like hours, stopping only to catch our breath and rehydrate ourselves. I remember thinking to myself, "I could live with this feeling. This could be my forever. I'd be more than happy if these were the last lips to ever kiss me, the last fingers to ever touch me. This would be happiness."

It was dark by the time we decided we were too depleted to keep going, and we were starving. I knew there were no restaurants close by but remembered a couple of street food vendors from the night before.

Luckily, they were there again. Cumin-roasted veggies, eggs, and meat. All halal, of course, and all on a stick. I found the broccoli particularly hard to eat and fumbled with my food. Alimu chuckled at me. "Having trouble?" he asked jokingly. I blushed, but Alimu smiled, picked up a whole stick of broccoli, and bit into it like a dog gnawing on a steak. "It's tough to eat," he said reassuringly. It wasn't the best of meals, but it satisfied us in a pinch. I was eager for an actual dining experience, something that wasn't processed and didn't come in a paper bowl. We didn't talk much that night, and Alimu didn't want to discuss the bear situation any further. He said it would be better the less I knew. Then we planned to get up early the next morning to catch the bus back to his hometown. We went to bed wrapped in each other's embrace. I inhaled the scent of sweat mixed with cologne and drifted off to sleep.

Chapter 10

The next morning arrived all too soon, and we quickly showered and packed my belongings up for the day's travel. We first needed to take a bus from the outskirts of the city into the city proper. We sat at the back of the bus, Alimu still dressed in black with his black face mask covering everything but his lightly hazel eyes. In China, it was not uncommon for people to wear the same winter outfit for multiple days in a row. In fact, many only had two or three full outfits that were rotated throughout the month in between washings. People just didn't sweat like westerners did, and they took great pride in keeping their clothes free of dirt and debris.

Alimu was paranoid about being recognized. He asked for the window seat, and he hunkered against the pane. After about thirty minutes, our bus came to a stop. It was a police checkpoint. As the police boarded the bus, I could feel Alimu begin to tremble. He scooted down in his seat until only his hair was visible to anyone looking from the front to the back, but the police didn't make their way to the back of the bus, and whatever or whoever they were looking for, they didn't find it. The two-minute ordeal was over, but Alimu remained stiff and silent for the rest of the ride into Xining.

Once in Xining, the bus dropped us off on what seemed to be a completely random street corner, but everybody disembarked, so I followed along. Alimu looked around and told me to wait. We couldn't take a taxi to the bus station because someone might recognize him, he told me. Instead, he trotted off and found a rickshaw driver. For twenty yuan, he took us to the bus station. Alimu told me to wait in the rickshaw for him. The driver and I shared a cigarette. Alimu smoked too, as I was pleased to learn. At least we could share in that habit. It took Alimu almost fifteen minutes to return, and he came bearing bad news. The snow in the mountains had gotten too dangerous for the buses to traverse, so there would be nothing going to or from Qilian that day. That meant no visiting his family in YangLong. I was so disappointed! But what about tomorrow, I asked, could we delay for a day? Alimu didn't have a clear answer. He said it's possible the snow could clear up in a day, but it's also possible it could persist for a week, and everybody would be stuck for a while. We decided it would be best if we got a hotel in Xining and just enjoyed our time together while we still could.

I could tell Alimu was bummed, and he apologized to me for not being able to take me to his mountains to see his yaks. But—he assured me—we would have plenty of time in the future. There would be more opportunities for visits in the warmer months. At least we were together now, so the trip wasn't all a waste. I agreed we should make the most of it while we still could, and asked the rickshaw driver if he knew of any hotels that would take foreigners. "Don't worry about it," Alimu said, "I know where to go." He gave the driver directions.

The hotel looked more like an oversized three-story house than a hotel. It was made of pure concrete that was painted a pink salmon color. Walking inside, the entryway was cramped, with four steps up to a small reception desk that was big enough to hold a computer, a keyboard, and a stack of papers. Alimu spoke to the desk attendant for some time. They spoke in *Qinghai Hua*, so I couldn't understand what they were saying, but the desk attendant kept looking at me and nodding. Eventually, Alimu handed over an unknown number of hundred-yuan bills, and we were given the keys to our room. Alimu led me up the stairs and through a winding hallway. There were wide, open windows on either side of the hallway, although they were not windows to the outside. Rather, they were windows to the inside of the rooms. The carpeted floor creaked beneath our feet as we made our way through the labyrinth of halls, taking another flight of stairs up before finally reaching our destination. Inside, there was a queen-sized bed, a nightstand, a dresser, an old boxy television, a tea kettle, an ashtray, and a bathroom with two towels and one toothbrush.

Immediately, Alimu closed the windows and drew the curtains shut. We then took off our coats and shoes and made ourselves comfortable on the bed. The place was pretty dingy, but the quality of places in China varied exceedingly depending on where you were. I thought perhaps Xining was just a poorer city, or perhaps Alimu didn't have enough money for a fancy hotel. Either way, I wasn't bothered by the decrepit feel of the place. At least Alimu was comfortable. He placed his face mask down on the nightstand, found his cigarettes in his jacket pocket and retrieved two. He handed one to me then extended his arm out to hold the lighter. I leaned in and the cigarette caught flame easily. These were LanZhou cigarettes, commonplace around western China, but hard to come by in Jinan. They pulled easily and were smooth, yet full-bodied. As we smoked, Alimu took out his phone and showed me more pictures of his family.

I asked to take a picture of him and me together. He hesitated, but agreed, under the conditions that I not post it online. He explained that in his faith, it's bad luck to share pictures with strangers, because pictures contain a pathway into the soul. Some Hui, he went on, avoid having their pictures taken altogether, but these were generally the elderly or extremely devoted. It was okay to share with friends and family because they knew what you looked like already and couldn't steal your soul. So, while I could take the picture and use the picture for personal reasons, he didn't want it spread to people he didn't know. This wasn't the first time I'd heard of people believing that pictures could affect the soul, although what I'd previously heard was the belief that pictures could actually trap one's soul if they weren't careful. Still, we leaned in close and I snapped a photo. He looked ruffled and exhausted, but happy. I had the biggest grin on my face, my head leaning against his shoulder while my dreadlocks poured over our bodies.

"What do you want to do now?" I asked.

"Well, I certainly know what I'd *like* to do," he said, and pulled me close again, holding my face while he kissed me.

We didn't put our clothes back on until it was time for supper. We didn't spend the entire time making love, of course, rather we were just completely comfortable while completely naked. In fact, I'd never felt so comfortable around anyone before. I felt like I could just exist in his presence and be perfectly content. We talked about religion and politics, the state of our countries, and about everything else and nothing at all. Eventually, it came time for dinner. Alimu told me he would take care of it, put his clothes back on, adjusted his face mask, and instructed me to wait for him. More waiting! I really wanted to go with him, but he insisted it would be easier if he went alone, and not to worry, he'd find something delicious.

He came back with more cumin-roasted barbeque, although this time there was a variety of tasty tofu to go along with the stubborn broccoli. I wasn't feeling very impressed, but I was hungry. I would have given anything for an actual meal, but Alimu's paranoia was seeping from his pores, and I didn't want to push him past his comfort level. We sat on the bed to eat, as there were no tables or chairs in the hotel room. We were surprised to find that our old TV had access to movies on demand, and Alimu became overly excited to find Rambo.

"I love Rambo!" he exclaimed. "It's my favorite movie!"

Except there was a minor problem... this was not Rambo, but rather Son of Rambo. Alimu was disappointed and turned the TV off entirely.

After dinner, we crawled back into bed with each other. What else could we do? We couldn't go outside, and there was nothing to do inside. So, we talked. And laughed. And kissed. On repeat, for hours. At one point, I remember playing with Alimu's hands, tracing the lines on his palms and the scars across his fingers.

"You have pretty rings," I said. He had three: two on each ring finger and one on his left index finger. "In my culture, you wear a ring on this finger when you're married." Chinese married couples didn't traditionally wear rings.

Alimu chuckled. "I know," he said, "but I like this one because it's the prettiest. It's real gold, too! See?"

He took his ring off and handed it to me. I tried to hold it up to the light to see it better, but I can hardly tell real gold from pyrite, so I just took him at his word. As I handed his ring back, he slipped off the other two.

"I want you to have these," he said. "It's too early to be engaged or married, but it would make me happy to give these to you. That way you'll always be reminded of me when we're apart."

"How about just one of the rings?" I suggested. "I think both would be too much for my hands."

I handed back one of the rings. The one I kept was thick and silver with an onyx-black gem in the center. The cut of the gem made it glimmer every way I rotated my hand. It was a very manly ring, and unless I had heard wrong, it was essentially serving as a promise ring. I found the gesture to be absolutely adorable, and it made me fall for him all the more. I knew things were moving fast, but we'd both taken a dive for each other, plunging straight into each other's hearts. It felt like the stars had collided and our bodies were the result of all the radiation and light that comes along with exploding entities. We were beaming for each other, and the last thing I wanted to do was to leave him the next day. If we had gone to YangLong, I would have changed my plane tickets, but neither of us had the cash needed to just hang out in a hotel for a week.

I needed to catch my plane, and Alimu needed to get back home while keeping a low profile. My flight was early the next morning, and I needed to be at the airport before eight a.m. This meant catching a cab by seven a.m. at the latest, which meant waking up at six a.m., which meant going to bed early. Sleep came easy for Alimu that night, and I laid awake listening to his soft snoring, watching his chest steadily rise and fall with each breath. I don't know what time sleep found me that night, but my dreams were fraught with nightmares. I woke up in a cold sweat with Alimu still asleep beside me. At least I hadn't done anything weird. Still, I just couldn't regulate myself to get any meaningful rest. I tossed and turned for the few remaining hours before my alarm clock sounded, then woke up Alimu.

We both got dressed silently, not wanting to be the first one to start the long string of goodbyes we were sure to utter. Alimu helped me pack. Then he straightened the hotel bed sheets and held my coat up for me. I let him help me put it on. "I can't take you to the airport," he said, "but I'll get you in a cab." With that, we left our dingy little hotel room behind and walked outside. The winter air was sharp and brisk, cutting deep to the bones with every gust of wind. Alimu hailed a taxi, and we held each other in a long embrace before he opened the backseat door for me.

"I'm going to miss you," I told him sadly.

"I'm going to miss you too, Anna," he replied, "but I promise we'll see each other soon."

And with that, I was on my way to the airport and back to Jinan.

Chapter 11

When I arrived back in Jinan, the city was almost empty. This was still the middle of the Spring Festival, and everyone who wasn't a Jinan native had returned home to see their loved ones. Most shops were closed or had limited hours, and it was considerably difficult to find a taxi. Samm was still gone, so I spent my days with my friend Katherine.

Katherine was an American from upper-class Chicago. She was a teacher at my former English training school, and when we met, we were instant friends. Katherine knew all my drama, and I knew all of hers. In previous years, we would hang out all the time, as if we were attached at the hip. This was before I left for a different training school and enrolled back into university. However, we still saw each other almost every Sunday or Monday when the English teachers got their weekends. Katherine was happy that I'd found someone who made me happy, but she wasn't very impressed by Alimu overall. "So, he's a yak herder? That's all he does all day—herd yaks?"

Katherine was insistent that I should find myself a well-educated, world-experienced person to hitch my wagon to and believed that a peasant from the mountains in the middle of nowhere just wasn't worth my time. While it's true that Alimu wasn't educated and wasn't well traveled, he offered me a sense of adventure and wonder that I just hadn't found anywhere else. It's not like I went looking for him; he just showed up one day. But at the time, Katherine wasn't fond of Muslim men in general. She previously spent a few years in Cairo where she went through a series of harrowing experiences that highly jaded her opinion. She didn't want me falling into a pit of misogyny, which was already rampant in China.

Regardless, Alimu's and my relationship continued to progress. We had fallen head over heels for each other, and I would race to get home on our designated phone call nights, just so I could hear his voice. I wore his ring with pride everywhere I went. After meeting in person, Alimu shared my WeChat ID with his half-brother and sister-in-law, and they, too, took a deep interest in me. His sister-in-law, Qiong, was especially talkative. She wanted to know everything about me and what I did during my day. I reciprocated the interest, and soon considered her to be something more than just an acquaintance but still less than a true friend. I was excited at the prospect of meeting her in person one day but decided that I needed to hold back a little, since everything I told her got back to Alimu. I had already slipped up once and told her that Alimu and I had slept together, but she had asked directly, and I couldn't see any reason to lie. She was younger than us, but she and her husband, Kelimu, seemed worldly enough to handle the information. Alimu wasn't happy that I'd told her about our business. In fact, it upset him greatly.

Nevertheless, we all moved past it, and Qiong grew on me to the point that I considered her a real friend. She told me how much Alimu talked about me, and we clucked away like hens talking about all the drama in our lives. Additionally, Qiong was not Muslim. Nor was she actually married to Alimu's half-brother. They just considered themselves married because they'd been engaged since high school. At first, Alimu's family didn't approve of their relationship because she was neither Hui nor Muslim, but they gradually accepted her as the years went by and she agreed to wear a headscarf while visiting the family home. She told me I would probably have to do the same if our relationship kept progressing, at least while visiting, although they might make an exception for me since I was a foreigner. I told her I didn't mind wearing one as a sign of respect. The Hui women all had such beautiful headscarves, anyway. I'd be lucky to have something so fashionable, I thought to myself.

Since coming back from Jinan, Alimu and I had been scheming up ways for him to move to my city. I would have been content with just a visit first, but Alimu insisted that he should move as soon as possible to be with me. We could share an apartment, he said, and he'd find work that would allow him to spoil me. The thought of living with Alimu excited me. I was ready for it. At this point, Alan had found his own apartment to move into, and I was struggling to keep up with the rent. My hours at work were also scheduled to be cut once summer break started, so I could use an extra person's income in the household.

One day, Alimu came to me with an idea. All he needed to do was buy a lorry, a truck! With that, he could contract out his truck to individuals and small businesses; it happened all the time in China. He would make good money that way. It didn't need to be anything too big, just enough to hold a decent number of items for inter-city transport. It truly was a brilliant idea, and Alimu was already business-savvy from a few other ventures. All he needed, he told me, was fifty thousand yuan to buy the truck. He asked me to help him. The sooner he could buy the truck, the sooner he could come to Jinan, and the sooner our lives together would start. But fifty thousand yuan was a lot of money, at least five months' worth of salary for me, or a whole year's salary if I was getting cut down to part-time. I just didn't have it, but he begged me for a solution. I told him I'd see what I could do. I immediately started saving my money, and Alimu assured me he was doing the same.

In May, my visa was set to expire as the school's summer break began. Needing to exit the country, I decided to take a trip back home. My work agreed to pay for the plane ticket in advance, contingent on me working off the cost after returning to Jinan. I agreed. It had been years since I was last home. However, what should have been two weeks filled with joyous reunion instead turned into immense pressure. Alimu told me that he found the perfect truck, but the seller would only hold it for him for a month. If we could just get the funding before then, everything would be all right. It would work out. He could make up the money to repay me in no time. What if I asked my parents?

Looking back, I believe the stress Alimu put on me about getting him a lorry pushed me into another hypomanic episode. Of course, I didn't know this information at the time, but I was acting recklessly and with little regard for the consequences of my actions. All I could focus on was Alimu at all costs.

I knew my parents weren't going to just give me almost seven thousand USD. Still, I thought, they might give me half of that. I would need a good story, though. I couldn't just tell them I needed money to buy my boyfriend a lorry—they'd never go for that. So, I cooked up a tale. I told them that my landlord was going to kick me out of my apartment unless she got six months' worth of rent up front. I very rarely lied to my parents. I hid very few things about my life from them, and I'd never really gotten into trouble as a teen. My parents had no reason not to believe me, and I put on a good show. I cried and begged for their help. I don't know if they saw through my ruse, or if they just wanted me to work through the hard parts of life of my own, but they didn't give me the money. I hope now they saw through the lies and knew something was amiss with my story.

I didn't stop with my parents. Once they rejected my proposition, I turned to my friends. I messaged everyone I could think of for money. I told them all the same story about getting kicked out of my apartment soon, and that if they could just help me out a little, it would all add up and I'd be okay. Absolutely nobody went for it. Maybe I wasn't believable. Maybe nobody had the money. It was certainly out of character for me to be begging, and I later came to learn that several people thought that my accounts had gotten hacked, and a scammer was posing as me to elicit funds. Out of all the mistakes I've made in my life, I'm most embarrassed about this one, lying to my family and friends about needing money. I truly lowered myself to something prideless and vulgarly exposed. And every day, Alimu would push a little harder. "Please, I know you're so smart, you can think of something!" he'd say.

I didn't pay as much attention to my family and friends stateside as I should have while I was home. I must have seemed like a terrible wreck. In truth, I wanted to stay with my family a little longer, as I had missed them so dearly, but changing the plane tickets was too expensive, and I needed to get back to my cats. Now, many of my friends in Jinan thought differently of me after my brief journey as a beggar, and people pulled away from me. As a result, I leaned harder into Alimu, and he was there to catch me emotionally. Still, the deadline to purchase his truck was drawing closer and closer with each passing day, and I was powerless to help the man I now loved.

Chapter 12

A few days after returning to Jinan, I made a new friend. I had met a man on the streets who was interested in the lives of foreigners in China and wanted to learn how to speak better English. His English was mediocre, so he was hoping to use me as practice. I added him as a QQ friend. I generally reserved QQ for strangers and passing acquaintances, while my WeChat account was for people I'd known for a while and would most likely see again. One night, when my QQ notification chimed and I was feeling particularly down, my new friend, Da Zhang, asked me how my day was going. I couldn't respond positively.

He wanted to know what was going on with me and why I was so glum. So, I told him the story of Alimu and how my dearly beloved desperately needed a lorry, but I was unable to help him, which meant he was probably never going to move to Jinan or that we would be delayed for a significant amount of time. Da Zhang asked me to wait a minute and went silent. He returned roughly ten minutes later and had news for me.

"I can help you with the money," he said.

"What?" I exclaimed. "You can help me with that much money? But you hardly even know me!"

"I believe in the power of love," he said. "But it's true that I don't know you. So, I'm going to require something big as collateral. I'm sure you can understand."

"The only big item I have is my laptop," I replied.

"No, I don't want that," he said.

"Then what do you want?" I asked.

"Your passport," he replied.

My passport... there was no way I could turn over my passport! What if I needed to travel? Still, Alimu kept telling me that once he had his lorry, he could make up the fifty thousand yuan and pay me back within a month. It would be easy money, he said. Da Zhang said the same thing, that lorry drivers could even make more money than that if they stayed busy enough. I mulled it over for an hour or so, weighing the pros and cons of the situation. I didn't need to travel anywhere anytime soon, and if I did need to go someplace, I could always just take a long-distance bus. That didn't require a passport. Moreover, most train stations would be okay with just a photocopy of your passport since all they really wanted was the number for identification purposes. I took Da Zhang up on his offer.

The next day, I made several photocopies of my passport and met Da Zhang at his house. He drew up a contract for me to sign that outlined the details of our transaction. I was to pay him back within six months' time, lest my passport would be forfeited completely. Until then, he would hold onto it. I didn't want to think about what he would do with it if I couldn't repay him. I signed the papers, then handed over my passport to what was essentially a complete stranger. In return, Da Zhang handed me the money in bright red one-hundred-yuan bills. I tried to count in my head how many days' worth of travel would be needed to drive across the country. Three? Maybe four? I felt a little uneasy about the risk I was taking, but the extended hypomania kept me convinced that I was making the best decision of my life. I thanked Da Zhang profusely and practically ran home.

I immediately contacted Alimu.

"I got the money!" I shouted over the phone.

Alimu was ecstatic, "Oh thank the heavens! Just in time! The dealer just called and told me tomorrow was my last day! Quick, send it over!"

Then he hesitated. "How did you get so much money so quickly?" he asked.

"I bartered my passport for it," I said, "but don't worry, I'll get it back as soon as you pay me back. It's just temporary."

"You shouldn't have done that," he scolded, "I never asked you to do that. Your passport is important."

"It's already been done," I said and asked for the best way to send him the funds. He gave me the information for his nearest Western Union, and later that day, he picked up the money. Maybe he wasn't happy that I'd leveraged my passport, but he certainly didn't reject the payment.

"I'll get the truck today," he texted, "and I'll start packing."

Three days later, I got the call from Alimu that he was on his way to Jinan. It was all I could think about. Lounging on Katherine's couch, I looked up just how long of a drive it was. The quickest route was a little over 1,200 miles, or about 22 hours driving. Alimu told me that he was only going to stop for the occasional break, meals, and sleep. So, that left about eight hours of driving per day, which meant that he should be in Jinan in four days' time, five at the most. Alimu was driving to Jinan with a friend to keep him company on the journey, and his friend had business to attend to in the city. He would fly back on his own later. I was grateful that Alimu would have the company, and thought that if they took turns driving, they might actually be here much sooner than anticipated.

But Alimu was strangely quiet during his journey to Jinan. I tried not to bother him, knowing that he couldn't focus on both me and the road at the same time, but I expected some sort of communication from him at night. Instead, I got next to nothing. I would receive messages such as "we're still on the road" or "I'll be there in a few days", but after days of knowing nothing else, I was feeling frustrated. Why wouldn't he tell me where in China they'd driven to that day? And why wasn't he coming online at night? It seemed like he would sporadically pop online to tell me that he's still traveling then immediately leave again. I was completely in the dark, and I didn't like the feeling.

Six days passed. But the only information I could get from him was "I'm still on the road." I told him I just didn't understand what was taking him so long to get here and why he wouldn't tell me where he'd gotten to by now. He told me that it was taking an exceptionally long time for them to drive across the country because the truck was so slow. "When you see it, you'll understand right away," he said. He also assured me that he was close, and that he'd be in Jinan by the next night. Finally! After nearly a week of waiting, Alimu would be here. I had gone through great lengths to get my apartment ready for him, deep cleaning and rearranging until it all looked perfect. I'd even planned a fancy dinner for him when he got here and stocked up on halal meat to cook with.

Still, by the next night, Alimu wasn't in Jinan. He wasn't online, either. I'd heard from him earlier in the day, and he confirmed that he would reach Jinan before ten p.m. Tense with anticipation, I could barely keep myself contained. But the longer I waited, the more worried I became. I envisioned all sorts of deadly car crashes in my head and wondered if anyone would contact me if he died. That night, I forced myself to turn off my phone and cried myself to sleep, hoping for better news tomorrow.

Another grueling two days went by before I got a call from Alimu. I immediately demanded to know where he was and what he was doing. I was angry.

"Calm down," he said, "and I'll tell you everything."

I took a deep breath.

"We had made it to Shandong," he started, "when we decided to stop for dinner. In order to celebrate, my co-driver ordered a bottle of baijiu. He poured me a glass and–"

"Wait, I thought you don't drink?" I interjected.

"I usually don't," he continued, "but he was really pressuring me, saying that we'd made it so far, and it was a celebration. He practically begged me to drink a glass with him. So, I did. He wanted me to drink more, but I was already feeling drunk and declined him. I don't know how much he drank."

He went on. "It was my friend's turn to drive, and I closed my eyes and tried to get some sleep. The next thing I knew, we were getting pulled over by the police! You see, my friend was actually drunk and he was driving all over the road. And since we were both drunk, they charged us both with drunk driving."

At this point in China, laws about drinking and driving were rapidly changing. Under Deng XiaoPing, drunk drivers were often tolerated. It was not unusual for afternoon business lunches to end in bottles of baijiu, and for attendees to drive back to work after drinking. Weekday afternoons and weekend evenings were notorious for their drunk drivers. Under Xi JinPing, however, new laws had been established and one could get into serious trouble, even lose his or her license if the offense was considered egregious enough. Additionally, those who were in the vehicle with a drunk driver could be considered co-conspirators, as it was their civic duty to refuse to ride in a car with a drunk driver and instead try to stop the driver from ever getting into his car.

But that still didn't explain why Alimu wasn't in Jinan. If he was arrested in Shandong, shouldn't he be somewhere in Shandong?

"Where are you?" I asked. "Are you in jail?"

"No, I'm not in jail," he replied, "but the police officers said they couldn't prosecute us in Shandong because we're not from the province, and they forced us to return to Qinghai. I've been on a train headed back. We had to pay for the truck to be towed home, too. I'm back at my home now."

Back at his home! Back in YangLong! So, we'd gone through all of this for nothing?! But they had gotten so close! Alimu had made it to my province, his feet were on Shandong soil, we were mere hours from holding each other, and now? Now it had all been thrown away because of drinking and driving. Why did they have to be so stupid! Still, I couldn't help but feel bad for Alimu.

"So, when will you be able to make it back to Jinan?" I asked.

"I don't know," he replied, "I used all my money getting the lorry towed back to me. It'll be a few months before I can save up enough for the trip out there again…unless you can help." This time, I couldn't help. I didn't have any money in savings, and the money I was earning needed to go towards getting my passport back, on top of rent and living expenses. And my salary had been cut almost in half by now, as the school was still waiting to recruit new students after the summer break. A pit of despair formed in my stomach, and I tumbled into it like the last leaf from an oak tree falling to the ground. What were we going to do now?

Chapter 13

The truth is, there wasn't much to do except wait. Alimu and I continued on as we had before, although now I couldn't pay for his phone minutes as often, meaning that we spent most of the time communicating via text. Then, on an unusually cool June night during a round of cheap wine and good music with Katherine, I received a text message from Alimu. I sat up straight in my chair.

"Anna, I'm going to go away for a while. You won't be able to reach me," read the message.

"What do you mean?" I asked. "Going where? Doing what? Why and for how long?"

"I have to go up on the mountain," he replied.

"But you go up on the mountain every day," I pushed.

"This time it's different. I'm going to harvest *chongcao*, and there's no service," he said. I had never heard of *chongcao* before, but a quick internet search revealed their secrets. *Chongcao* was a caterpillar fungus, also known as cordyceps. Alimu was going to make a lot of money harvesting these if it was a good year. They were considered quite an expensive delicacy that could do anything from helping with a cough to curing cancer. He said he would only be gone for a week, and not to worry because he'd be back soon. What else could I do besides say "okay" and wish him well? I didn't want him to go, but he was a busy man with his own life to lead, and I was a busy woman who didn't need to be tied to a man every day of my life. Wasn't I? So, I said goodbye to him knowing that it would be the last time I'd hear from him for days on end. Again. The wine flowed freely that night.

But two days later, Alimu appeared online again. Like many other chat clients, QQ displayed when a friend was online, inactive, or busy. I tried to reach out to him, but received no answer in response. Shortly after that, he was offline once more. He reappeared again later that night. I reached out, but again received no answer. Now I was feeling annoyed. Wasn't he supposed to be out of service range? If he had service, why was he ignoring me? The next day, he was online when I woke up. After still receiving no response from him by that afternoon, I sent a rather scathing message about being ignored.

"I'm not Alimu," the response read.

"What do you mean you're not Alimu? This is his QQ!" I typed back furiously.

"He's not here. I'm his friend," read the message.

"Well, where is he then?" I asked.

"I don't know, he told me I could use his QQ," typed the stranger.

I tried to elicit more information from whoever was on the other end of the conversation, but I received no more responses. What did he mean Alimu let him use his QQ? Why would anybody want to use someone else's QQ, why not just make your own account? It's not like the app cost money! Is this something that's temporary, or did Alimu mean for him to use it forever? All I could do was wait and see. The rest of the week passed, and Alimu's account came online sporadically across the days. Any further messages I sent to him were ignored. Then two weeks passed, and I still had no word from Alimu. Any time I asked Qiong about Alimu's location, she told me she didn't know where he was, except that he said he was going to go harvest the cordyceps.

By now, I was feeling very concerned. This wasn't the first disappearing act that Alimu had performed, but it was by far the longest. Before, he always came back with a good reason for his absence. I was worried that something had gone extremely wrong. I voiced my concerns to Qiong one night, and she asked to call me so we could speak directly. I agreed. It took time for us to get used to each other's accents, but we soon found a natural flow of listening intently and speaking slowly. She asked me to tell her exactly what was going on between Alimu and I, and how long it had been since I'd last seen him. So, I told her everything that had happened since returning from Xining. Qiong didn't indicate any shock or surprise at the mention of the lorry purchase, but rather seemed like she knew all about it. Of course she would if it was all true. I found that reassuring. She then told me to hang on while she talked to Kelimu about something. She'd call me back.

My phone rang about an hour later. It was Qiong. She told me that if I could come out to Xining, they would take me to go see Alimu. I told her I would love to do that, but I couldn't afford the train tickets. She told me that she and Kelimu would be willing to pay for that, but I needed to cover the other expenses like cab fare and food for the journey. It was a two-day train ride, and I'd need to bring my own supplies. I readily agreed, and with my schedule being open, we chose train tickets that left for Xining the next day.

Unfortunately, there were no high-speed bullet trains that went to Xining. To get there by train, it would have to be a slow train. Altogether, it was a forty-two-hour journey. I was lucky that I had been able to snag a seat in a hard sleeper instead of having just a hard seat (the soft seats were all booked), or even worse, standing room only. The train was packed when we boarded. My hard sleeper cabin had a total of six beds, three bunks on either side, with a narrow passage in between the sets of beds that yielded just enough space for one to stand sideways while climbing up the bunks. The best of the hard sleeper seats were the bottom bunks. These were close to the ground, and you could sit up on your bed with just enough head space to avoid colliding with the middle bunk. This made it ideal for the rich and elderly.

The middle bunk was the next best bunk. You couldn't sit up very well in these bunks, but you still had enough space to move around on all fours. You also weren't too far off the ground, which made it ideal for middle-aged people and children. The worst bunks were the top bunks, which is the class of bunk I had. There was only about two and a half feet of space between the bed and the ceiling of the train car, and it took a bit of effort to get myself up into the bed using a series of small metal rungs that extended from the wall. Then I had to position my belongings somewhere. I'd brought only a backpack, but the space underneath the bottom bunks had already been taken, and I wanted my belongings close to me anyway. I formed a barrier between the foot-end of the bed and the wall of the cabin with my coat, to prevent anything from slipping in between the gap, and positioned my backpack in the far corner of the bed. I accomplished this all while army-crawling around the bed.

I tried to use my phone as little as possible, only turning it on to check the time every couple of hours. Although there were charging stations on the train, they were mostly located in the upper-class cabins with the soft sleepers. Those cars only had four beds to a cabin, were nicely padded, and had two outlets for electronics. The hard sleepers were thinly padded with no electrical outlets. For that, I would need to find an outlet next to a seat in the aisle that ran along the outside of the cabins. These seats were almost always occupied, as the train was completely packed and it was a first-come, first-serve situation. Every now and then, I would climb down from the top bunk to stretch my legs and look out the window. The floors of the train were caked in stubborn black dirt from thousands of shoes, and the squatty-potty toilets were flooded with urine that was constantly tracked outside the bathrooms. It was imperative to constantly wear shoes if I wasn't in my bunk, and I quickly learned how to tie my laces while still laying down.

I saw the most beautiful scenery in those two days. I was intensely struck by one stretch of land in particular, although I have no idea which part of the country we were traveling through at the time. The railway ran across a high double-bridge. Below the bridge raged a deep but muddy brown river. Steep, forested mountains rose up on either side of the river, and a small town perched in between the valleys and the water that flowed through them. As our train chugged along, high above this scene, I felt like I was in a fairytale. I was a classic adventurer leaving her small town to see the big, wide world for the first time.

I had brought along a bit of food, mostly just instant noodles and bread snacks, but was more interested in the meals the train attendants had for sale. During mealtimes, the attendants would roll carts of pre-plated food through the aisles of the train cars, shouting out the names of the dishes and the price. Twenty yuan would buy you a meal that was plenty enough to feed you, although a bottle of water would cost extra. I would have to eat my meals lying down, though, and keep the juice-riddled trash next to me until the attendants came around once more to gather refuse. When I wasn't eating or walking around the train cars, I was smoking. I brought along four packs of cigarettes for the two-day long trip, and I smoked every single one of them. Like always, it was great for making conversation, but the ashy taste in my mouth soon became too much to stomach.

That left reading and sleeping as the only other alternatives. My book was a collection of short stories, so my routine became reading a story, then taking a nap, then reading a story, then taking a nap, until it was either time to smoke, eat, or stretch my legs again. Overall, the trip really wasn't as horrible as I'd anticipated. It's amazing how much one can sleep when there's truly nothing else left to do. Somewhere around the thirty-eight-hour mark, I messaged Qiong with my arrival time. She assured me that she and Kelimu would be there to receive me. I tried to freshen up as much as possible, but changing my clothes and brushing my teeth required straddling the urine-soaked floor of the bathroom and silently praying that the lurch of the train wouldn't cause me to slip. Despite the difficulties, I managed to look and smell decent before the train pulled into the Xining railway station.

I left the train with the mass of passengers and made my way through the exit hall. Standing near the doors, I looked around. How was I supposed to find them in all these people? They could be anywhere, and since they didn't like posting pictures of themselves, I'd only seen what they looked like a handful of times. Suddenly, I felt a hand reach out and grab my arm.

"Anna, there you are!" It was Qiong. She pulled me close to her and squeezed my elbow. She was just slightly taller than I was, with thick, long black hair that cascaded down her shoulders. She wore her black lace headscarf in a manner that still exposed most of her hair (but not the top of her head), a white ruffled blouse, and jeans. Next to her stood another very petite woman. She was shorter than both of us, extremely slender, and wore an elaborate white and floral headscarf with her hair in a bun to give the presentation of more volume. Her clothes draped around her, a long and loose-fitting floral shirt, a sheer duster, and black leggings.

"I'm Su'erdai," she said, "I'm Alimu's sister." I nodded and smiled to her, suddenly feeling rather shy.

"Kelimu is waiting for us in the car," Qiong said. "Let's go!"

Wasting no time, Qiong picked up my backpack while Su'erdai slipped her arm around mine and started to lead me towards the exit. I tried to protest Qiong's taking of my bag, since it was so heavy, but I knew it would be useless. She was being polite, trying to treat her guest well. I felt a little uncomfortable with Su'erdai hanging on to me like she was, but this was common among female friends, and again, she was just attempting to treat me well. Outside, a car pulled up to meet us at the sidewalk, and we all climbed in. Kelimu was in the driver's seat, and he turned around to greet me with a big smile. Kelimu was taller than all of us but still very slender. He wore a close-fitting button-up shirt and black skinny jeans. Just when I was contemplating how his square jaw complimented his boxy haircut, I suddenly realized that everyone in the car was staring at me.

"You're so pretty," Su'erdai said.

"You really are!" Qiong exclaimed. "And I love your hair!"

I thanked them for their kind words and offered a few of my own in return.

"Oh, we have to take her to Yonus!" Qiong suddenly cried. I wondered who Yonus was.

"Absolutely, I think he's waiting for us now," Kelimu answered.

"We're going to take you to a hotel, then we'll get you something to eat," Su'erdai told me.

We drove around the city to a mid-level hotel. It wasn't fancy, but it looked like an actual hotel this time, had a large reception area, and the rooms were spacious with two beds each. "We got three rooms," Qiong said, "one for just you, one for me and Su'erdai, and one for the boys!" I barely had enough time to set my belongings down on my bed before the group started into a commotion.

"Yonus, you're here!" called Su'erdai.

"Look, we got her! She's real," I heard Kelimu say.

The man who walked in was strikingly handsome, and resembled Alimu but softer. His hair wasn't as floppy as Alimu's, and his face was more rounded, but there was no denying that the two of them were closely related.

"This is Yonus," Qiong told me.

"I'm Alimu's brother!" Yonus exclaimed, sticking a hand up and waving. Alimu's brother grew up separately from the rest of his siblings. After their father passed away, their mother was left with three young children. Alimu had previously explained that since he was the oldest, he was capable of helping out with household duties. Su'erdai, on the other hand, was just a baby, and still needed her mother's constant attention. Yonus was too young to help and too old to be at his mother's breast, so at the young age of three, he was sent to live with his uncle. His uncle eagerly adopted Yonus and now considered him to be his son. When Yonus spoke of his father, he was referring to his uncle.

We all sat on the beds of my hotel room. I was surrounded by four very eager quasi-strangers, all looking right at me with big smiles on their faces, their bodies vibrating with excitement.

"Tell us everything about yourself!"

"Tell us everything about you and Alimu!"

"Yeah, and what has Alimu told you about us?"

The questions started flying at me faster than I could answer them. I told them everything Alimu had told me and showed them the photos that Alimu had shared with me. My favorite photo of Alimu, a picture of him running through the ocean surf, had a man running next to him, smiling in the sun.

"Is this you, Kelimu?" I asked.

"Nope, that's ME!" Yonus said proudly, pointing a finger at his chest.

I told them every important thing about myself that I could think of. It was most of the basics: where I came from, my family makeup, why I originally came to China, what I was doing in China now, and so on, but what they really wanted to know was more information about Alimu and me. How had we met? What were our plans? Were we in love with each other? Why wasn't he talking to me? And my personal favorite: YOU GAVE HIM HOW MUCH MONEY!? After each answer I gave, they would talk excitedly amongst themselves in *Qinghai Hua*, not caring to clue me in on what they were talking about. From what I could pick up on, they were talking about me and Alimu. I just couldn't tell if it was good or bad.

Suddenly, Qiong turned to me. "Anna, we're going to take you to dinner. Do you want to shower before we go?"

"I need to shower first, too," Yonus said, "I'm filthy from work."

With that, everyone cleared out to their respective rooms while those who wanted to clean themselves took the opportunity. The warm water felt refreshing after two days without even a wet wipe on the train. I wasn't sure if I should dress in my best clothes now or later; I wasn't sure when we were meeting Alimu. I decided to put my old clothes back on. They weren't dirty, as I'd been in them for only a few hours, and I only had a precious few days' worth of outfits with me.

I can't recall the dinner we had that night. Unfortunately, some parts of my memory are still blocked. The mind has a funny way of protecting us from what we want to know. I do, however, remember feeling full, and grateful that they paid for my meal. And I remember that it was an actual meal, eaten in a restaurant, rather than street food and cumin-coated broccoli. Afterwards, the group led me through Xining's night market. I still had no clue what our overall plan was. Nobody had told me anything, and for some reason it just felt rude to ask, as if I would be pushing instead of allowing myself to be an entertained guest.

We stopped at a clothes vendor, and Qiong rifled through the shirts until she stopped on a black, sleeveless top.

"*Ai!*" she exclaimed, "this would be perfect for you!" She held it up against my body, looking me and the shirt over.

"I don't think it will fit..." I protested. Most clothes in China didn't fit me.

"Nonsense, it will fit you just fine!" she insisted. "Here, try it on!"

I pulled the semi-sheer shirt over what I was wearing, expecting it to get stuck on my shoulders. But to my surprise, it slid right over my body and hung low like a tunic. It actually did look rather good on me, and both Qiong and Su'erdai insisted they would pay for it. They argued for a moment about who was going to hand over the cash, but eventually Qiong won out, handing over her money in front of a slightly sulking Su'erdai. Then, feeling tired from the day's excitement, we decided to head back to the hotel.

"Will we see Alimu tonight?" I asked sheepishly.

"No, not tonight," Qiong told me. "We still have to call for him. Tomorrow we'll drive to Qilian and tell him to meet us there."

"Don't you know where he is?" I questioned.

"No," Qiong responded, "but we know how to make him show up."

Chapter 14

We finally left Xining the next day around ten a.m. It was going to be a six-and-a-half-hour-long car ride before we reached the town of Qilian. There were toll roads, but no active checkpoints, meaning I could easily sneak into HaiBei county without fear of getting caught. Yonus did not join us. He lived and worked in Xining and had only wanted to meet me to see if I was real. He added me as a QQ friend before leaving the hotel and wished us on our way.

Since the car belonged to Kelimu, he was the designated driver. Qiong sat next to him in the passenger seat. I sat behind Qiong, and Su'erdai sat behind Kelimu. I watched as Su'erdai fidgeted with something under her headscarf.

"It's my hearing aid," she explained. "I got hit in the ear when I was little, and now I have a hard time hearing." I would later come to find out that the person who hit her had been her own stepfather. Alimu had alluded to his violent temper in the past, and it seemed that Su'erdai had received the brunt of his abuse.

The ride was mostly silent. We were all staring out of our respective windows. Occasionally, the three of them would talk amongst themselves. Other times, they would involve me in their conversations, asking me questions about myself or Alimu. I answered every question truthfully, figuring I had nothing to hide if I wanted to get to the bottom of where Alimu was. We took turns controlling the music, but I was more interested in the scenery that met me through the window more than anything else.

We first traveled north through MenYuan county. MenYuan was famous for its rapeseed fields that flowered bright yellow blossoms in the late spring and early summer. The biggest fields lie in valleys between expansive grass-covered mountains. Here, the mountains jutted up sharply, but only a few reached high enough to cross the snow line. Kelimu slowed the car dramatically on the switchback roads that traced the bodies of the mountains, but picked up speed along the mountains' spines. From MenYuan, the mountains began to slowly fold towards the ground, while the ground simultaneously climbed in altitude. We had climbed from 7,200 ft above sea level to over 11,000 ft, and at times it felt hard to breathe. Before long, the mountains began sloping upwards again, and the grasslands spread out at their feet. The whole world was wrapped in lush but low-lying grasses and baby-blue skies. Snow-capped mountains gave birth to gushing creeks, bursting with fresh meltwater. And I finally saw yaks for the first time.

I was surprised at how small the yaks were. We were stuck behind a herd that was attempting to cross the road without blocking traffic for too long. They were waist-high beasts that more so resembled a large breed of shaggy dog with horns. The big white yaks I'd seen in tv shows and magazines, as it turns out, were considered more ornamental here, used for tourists who want to snap a photo with a bona fide yak. However, the common yaks—the ones raised for their meat and milk—are considerably smaller, about three-and-a-half feet tall at the withers.

Qiong and Su'erdai had purchased a variety of snacks from the street vendors at the market the night before, so we didn't stop to eat. In fact, we didn't stop anywhere for the first three hours, until we reached the public toilet by the side of the road in Ebuzhen. A small concrete building on a raised platform, the toilet was only two open stalls with a hole in the floor that sat directly above a pit dug out below the structure. At least I'd remembered to bring my own toilet paper. Neither public nor private restrooms in China provided toilet paper for their users. After we'd all had a bit of relief and I'd taken the opportunity to smoke a cigarette, we climbed back in the car for the remaining handful of hours.

But something happened that made us slow down our pace dramatically. Perhaps Kelimu wasn't driving straight to Qilian. I didn't have the slightest idea where I was, really. Soon it fell dark, and the temperature dropped so dramatically that I regretted not bringing a jacket. With no houses or villages for miles on end and no streetlights to light the road, Kelimu had to open his door to properly see the road when we hit the switchback that would take us off the spine of the mountains and into the town of Qilian. By the time we reached a hotel in town that would barter to take a foreigner for the night, it was nearing eight p.m. Our six-hour journey had turned into a ten-hour journey, but I still don't know where those extra four hours came from.

It was even harder to breathe in Qilian. We had climbed to over 19,000 ft in elevation, and while Alimu's family was used to the thin air, my lungs struggled to feel full and my feet dragged getting out of the car. Our hotel room had three beds. Su'erdai laid claim to one, Qiong and Kelimu took another, and I took the bed closest to the window. Then the three of them gathered together and spoke in hushed voices. I couldn't understand what they were saying, but I could hear Alimu's name interspersed between their sentences. Finally, Kelimu took out his cell phone and made a call. The recipient answered right away, and I could hear it was Alimu! He picked up on the first ring for his brother, which meant he had cell service. Yet, he had still been ignoring *me*! Su'erdai told me to sit on the bed and wait because Alimu would be here soon. She gave an estimate of twenty minutes. I asked if Alimu had his lorry.

"Oh yes, he has that!" she replied, then asked, "Is this the same truck that you gave him money for?"

I confirmed that it was, and Su'erdai fell silent. She sat on her bed and pulled out her phone, occupying herself during the wait. An hour passed, and there was still no word from Alimu. They called him again, and again he promised to be there shortly. Twenty minutes, he said. I spent the next hour staring out the window that showed a view of the street below. I was watching each lorry that passed by, hoping that it would turn towards the hotel and park. None of them did, though. After waiting for nearly two hours, I heard Qiong exclaim, "He's here!"

Kelimu opened the hotel door without waiting for a knock, and in walked Alimu. He was dressed in his leather jacket and dark pants, gloves covering his hands. Qiong, Kelimu, and Su'erdai gathered around Alimu, and they began quietly arguing, not wanting to raise their voices and risk being overheard through the thin hotel walls. They stole occasional glances at me as they rapidly talked amongst themselves, until Alimu broke away from them and turned to me.

"Come with me," he said.

"Where are we going?" I asked.

"To talk. In private. We can sit in my car, now come on," he said firmly.

I followed him downstairs and outside to the parking lot where a compact car was parked. He opened the back seat and gestured for me to get in. Once I was inside, he closed the door before making his way around the back of the car and claiming the other back seat for himself.

"What are you doing here?" he asked softly.

"I'm looking for you!" I said rather angrily. "You've been gone for weeks, and I haven't heard anything from you! But you answer your brother's call like it's nothing, and your family didn't have any idea that you were planning to move to Jinan! What the hell is going on?"

"I told you I was going to be away for a while. I–" he began, but I interjected.

"You said you would be gone for a week! Not three!"

"I know," he said, "but things have gotten really busy, and all I do is work. I've been hauling things all over the province trying to make enough money to move to Jinan and pay you back. I was even working tonight when they called me." He gestured towards the hotel with his chin.

"But why didn't they know about you moving to Jinan?" I persisted.

"I wasn't going to tell them until I was already moved and settled. They don't have to know everything about my life," he said. "And I can't call or text while I'm driving, so that's why I haven't been talking to you."

"What about after work? It's easy to get on QQ before bed and say hello."

"You're right," he sighed, "I've just been so tired from all the heavy lifting and driving that all I can think about is sleeping. I don't want to talk to *anybody* at night, it's not just you. I'm not ignoring you, I'm just exhausted!"

I didn't know what to make of what he said. On the one hand, I felt like being tired was a pretty shitty excuse for not making at least some form of contact. Especially since I knew he had access to his phone and was in an area that had service. On the other hand, I felt guilty. Was I just being too possessive? Should I have just waited a little longer? Qiong and Kelimu said that they didn't know where Alimu was, either, yet they knew exactly how to get him to come out of hiding. Was he ignoring them, too? If he was ignoring everybody, that would give more credibility to his story, but it still wasn't very kind to just leave me in the dark. I stared at the floor of the car, not knowing what to say, mulling over everything Alimu had told me.

Then, he took my hand in his, and gently turned my face toward him.

"I've missed you so much," he spoke in a soft and gentle voice, "and I love you. We'll be together soon." Then he kissed me, and I kissed him back. Our hands groped at one another in the darkness as we tore away our most inconvenient articles of clothing and held each other close. There wasn't much space in the back seat of the car, but when two people are insistent on making love, they will always find a way. We were passionate, like we'd been separated for years instead of months, but it was quick. We knew the rest of Alimu's family were waiting for us.

"You're still wearing my ring," Alimu smiled at me while helping me shuffle my clothes back into a presentable fashion.

"Of course, I never take it off."

"Good," he said. "Keep wearing it."

We stayed inside the car to smoke our cigarettes, not wanting anyone to spot an illegal foreigner on the streets of Qilian at night.

"You really didn't need to come here," Alimu said calmly. "I'm not going to leave you. You just need to be patient. Let's go back in."

I nodded silently and followed him to the hotel entrance. "Don't tell my family any more about us. They're just going to gossip, and I like things more private," he said. "And absolutely don't tell them what we did in the car." He led me back to the hotel room and knocked on the door. Kelimu and Qiong answered together, and Alimu motioned for me to go inside. He didn't follow but instead stood in the doorway talking to his family. His tone was stern, and he shook a finger at Qiong, but he wasn't angry and he wasn't flustered. When he was done, he turned and walked away.

Immediately, Su'erdai came over to my bed. "What did he say to you?" she asked. I told her everything that had happened, except for the sex. She nodded her head as I spoke and seemed satisfied with my answer. "If he says to wait then all you can do is wait," she said. She then urged me to try to get some rest. Everybody was going to bed. We had to wake up early the next day if we were going to get to Xining before the next train left for Jinan.

We spent the ride to the city in silence. I was too busy staring out the window, half of the time feeling awestruck at my surroundings and the other half mulling over Alimu. I think everyone else was deep in thought, too. But it was late afternoon when we reached Xining, and we discovered there would be no more trains to Jinan until the next morning. Kelimu stopped the car at an intersection near a yellow building.

"Wait here," he said to me, "and Yonus will come get you."

He gave me Yonus's phone number, and they all wished me luck. I thanked them profusely for their help before they drove away. They still needed to get back to YangLong. I waited on the street corner for twenty minutes before Yonus met me. He had just gotten off work and had another man with him. He introduced him as Salihan, his cousin. They walked me to a nearby hotel and paid for my room. The room was barely big enough for a twin bed and a tv, but it would get me through until the next day. Then Yonus left to find me dinner.

Salihan stayed behind to keep me company. He sat on the floor next to me and handed me a cigarette from a bright red pack.

"You know Alimu is married, right?" Salihan said.

I was shocked and began to panic inside. However, I knew if I wanted good information, I would have to remain calm. I took a deep breath to settle my racing heart.

"What do you mean? How long has he been married?" I said sharply.

"Not long," Salihan replied. "Maybe a few months? But anyway, he has a wife."

A few months? A few months is how long we'd been together. How could Alimu possibly have a wife of a few months when he's out there telling me he's moving to Jinan? Was perhaps I the new wife Salihan was referencing?

"Ask him about it yourself," Salihan said, taking a long puff from his cigarette, "but don't tell him I told you."

Just then, Yonus returned with a bag of hot noodles. Finally, a meal! We hadn't had dinner the night before, nor breakfast that morning. I was so thankful! I held off on eating until we'd all said our goodbyes, then slurped all the noodles down in what felt like less than a minute. Feeling satiated yet frustrated, I decided to call Alimu and ask him if he really was married. I wanted to confront this information head on. I'd be damned if I'd let him make a fool out of me!

Alimu answered my phone call on the second ring. "I know you're married!" I stated harshly.

"What? I'm not married! Who told you that?" Alimu sounded upset.

"He told me not to tell you…"

"He? Who is he?" Alimu demanded loudly, then said more calmly, "Please tell me. I won't know how to fix this if you don't tell me who told you."

"Salihan," I said and waited impatiently for his response. It was not what I expected.

"That God-damned Salihan! I hate him! He's always making up drama! He's absolutely lying to you, and he lies all the time! Yonus likes to hang out with him, but I don't because he's always pulling stunts like this. Forget about Salihan! You can't trust him!" Alimu said, trying to hold back his anger.

"Fine," I said, "I trust you. It doesn't make sense, anyway."

"Just get yourself back to Jinan safely," he said. "And don't worry about what other people are saying. Remember, I love you. Now, I have to go, but we will talk soon."

"Okay, I love you too. Please call as soon as you can."

I felt better after hearing Alimu's explanation. Some people just live for drama, no matter where you are in the world. I *wanted* to believe Alimu, so I did.

Chapter 15

Back in Jinan, I still wasn't hearing from Alimu as much as I would have liked, but at least he was calling every other day or two. We would only talk for fifteen to thirty minutes, and Alimu always sounded stressed. I tried to keep reminding myself that he was busy making money for Jinan, for us, and that I needed to give him the space that he was asking for, but it was difficult. The infatuation and love I had for Alimu made me want to burst open at the seams and scream his name from the rooftops. I hated having to stifle the momentum we had spent all this time building.

I was able to keep my mind occupied by focusing much of my free time back on the karaoke group. There, we'd welcomed a new friend into the fold, and it just so happened that he lived close to Jinan, in a town about an hour away called ChangQing. His name was Muhaimai, and he was able to travel to Jinan frequently because he had his own car. He was married and owned his own LanZhou pulled noodle restaurant where he and his wife both worked, him as the noodle puller and her as the cook. Muhaimai knew all about my relationship with Alimu and that I'd spent the past few weeks since returning from Xining steeped in frustration. In an attempt to take my mind off of things, he invited me to spend a few days with him and his wife in ChangQing. I happily agreed, eager for an adventure.

The bus ride between Jinan and ChangQing was bumpy, which made it impossible to read. Luckily, I still had music to occupy my time on the two-hour journey. Buses were considerably slower than taking a hired car or taxi, but they were also considerably cheaper. Arriving in ChangQing around midday, I showed Muhaimai's address to a taxi driver who agreed to take me there for ten yuan. I agreed, even though the metered price would have been less. The noodle shop was on the outskirts of town, where dust lined the streets so thick, they looked like dirt roads. Lorries flew by day and night, on their way to the neighboring cities of LiaoCheng, Tai'An, and JiNing. Muhaimai and his wife greeted me warmly, and immediately insisted that I eat.

My favorite dish from the LanZhou noodle restaurants was stir-fried eggs and tomatoes served with knife-cut noodles, and Muhaimai's wife made an excellent rendition. I tried to help in the kitchen, but she shooed me away, insisting that she could manage on her own. While she was cooking, Muhaimai showed me where I would be sleeping. It was in their bed. In their bed! They lived upstairs from their noodle shop, in the small two rooms that held all their belongings. Their bed was in the furthest room, and was actually two queen-sized beds pushed together to make one big bed.

"You'll sleep over here next to this wall," Muhaimai said, "and my wife will sleep in the middle, and I'll sleep on the outside!" He seemed happy with this plan. It felt a little strange to me, but I didn't want to shun their hospitality. Sure, I could sleep in the same bed as a married couple, it would be fine! They're just other people, after all. I put my bag down on the bed and asked about the bathroom.

There wasn't one. If I wanted the bathroom, I would have to go to the public toilet house across the street. Oh boy. And it didn't have running water, so if I wanted to wash my hands, I'd have to take a bottle with me. So I gathered up my toilet paper and water bottle and trotted across the street to the bathroom. At least this one had a tile floor and ceramic toilets, but there was still urine soaking the floors from poor aim and carelessness. The hardest part about using a squatty-potty was balance. Sometimes, one would get lucky enough to find a toilet with a stall. Other times, the toilets were just porcelain holes in the ground with nothing to brace yourself against. The vast majority of westerners cannot squat comfortably. When they try, most find that the heels of their feet roll upwards, leaving only their toes to balance on. Without a wall to place a hand on for better balance, I tipped from side to side while I tried to pee. Luckily, I never toppled.

I spent the rest of the afternoon just sitting in Muhaimai's shop, watching him and his wife work. We all made good conversation with each other, and we found great amusement in watching the bewildered looks on the lorry drivers' faces as they walked in to find a foreigner sitting in a tiny noodle shop in a tiny dusty town. They closed the shop early that night, around seven p.m., and Muhaimai took off his taqiyya. He placed it on the table before bringing out a bottle of baijiu, a case of beer, and various bottled juices.

"It's disrespectful to wear it while I'm drinking," he explained, noticing that I'd been staring at his headpiece. "I don't drink around my family, but tonight is a special occasion!" His wife sat down next to me and opened a bottle of juice. She abstained from alcohol.

I asked if he had a deck of cards, and hearing my request, Muhaimai jumped out of his chair and bounded upstairs. He came back with three decks of cards. I grabbed the one that looked the most used. I taught them how to play a modified version of King's Cup, a game that I'd found my Hui friends group enjoyed greatly, even if they were only drinking water. After the game finished, his wife excused herself from the table.

"It's time for me to go to bed," she yawned, but insisted that Muhaimai and I stay up and keep talking.

The truth is, we had a lot to talk about. There was always plenty of drama going on in the karaoke groups, plus we had my issues with Alimu to talk about, and his issues with his wife's fertility. They desperately wanted a baby, and all the strange medical advice they kept getting just wasn't working. Adoption is an extremely unpopular choice in China, however, and they couldn't afford IVF treatments. They were starting to receive pressure from both of their families, and Muhaimai wondered if he could ever make his wife happy without a child. We talked long into the night about this topic, and it was past midnight before we eventually retired upstairs.

The next morning, I woke up to find both Muhaimai and his wife already busy at work, preparing the shop to open in an hour. They had let me sleep late, and it was close to nine-thirty in the morning. I didn't feel well, though. My stomach felt nauseous, and I was cramping like crazy. I felt my period starting. I knew it was coming, so I was prepared, and quickly dug out my sanitary products from my bag before running across the street to the toilet. Except when I pulled down my underwear, there was no blood. There was absolutely nothing there. Then I threw up.

"Oh no," I thought to myself. "This isn't happening, is it?" I pulled my pants back up without peeing and ran back across the street.

"Muhaimai!" I shouted. "Where can I find a pregnancy test?!"

"The store down the street sells them," he said, pointing down the road to the left.

I bought one. It was just a small strip in a box with a tiny collection cup for urine. I couldn't read the instructions, but luckily, they had pictures that showed what to do.

I jogged back to the public bathroom and made a complete mess of myself trying to piss into the tiny, dented urine collection cup. I dipped the stick in, placed it gingerly on the floor, then waited, as so many women do, to learn my fate.

It was positive.

Chapter 16

I couldn't keep myself from smiling. I was terrified, as this was the last thing I needed, but I took great comfort in knowing this was Alimu's baby. It felt like everything was going to be all right. We would work through it all together. He loved me, and I loved him, and we didn't need anything else in the world. Except maybe this baby. Then we would be complete. I felt so bad, however, walking back into Muhaimai's shop, knowing that they've been struggling to conceive for so long, and here I was pregnant without even trying.

"Are you pregnant?" Muhaimai asked.

I nodded my head, and a smile spread across his face. He was happy for me.

"What are you going to do about it, then?" asked Muhaimai. "You're not even married."

"I don't know," I responded, "but I want to keep it."

"Well, in the meantime, you need to start eating food for a pregnant woman," Muhaimai said, and he called for his wife to make me a dish of fried eggs and wood-ear mushrooms. She hurried herself about the kitchen and said nothing to me about my pregnancy. I couldn't blame her, though. She was going through several daily regiments of Chinese traditional medicine for her infertility, and she'd become disheartened. I ate everything she cooked and thanked her profusely.

On the bus ride back home, I kept mulling over the best way to tell Alimu that I was pregnant. Should I send a text? No, that's too impersonal, and I want to hear his reaction. Should I call him? I didn't want to inconvenience him while he was working. I decided it would be best to wait until he called me. That would be a guaranteed moment of downtime for him, and he could really enjoy the news that way. Still, I wanted to tell Samm right away, and her I could text. I couldn't wait any longer. I had to tell someone!

Samm was supportive but worried. After all, I wasn't well-off financially, didn't have a full-time job, and having a baby would change everything about life in China. I could no longer be a carefree spirit drifting wherever the wind and spring water takes me, I'd have to step up and be a mom. It was daunting to imagine, but I had full confidence that the Universe would find a way to make everything all work out okay, and all I had to do was put my trust and faith in myself and my own power. As it goes, surprise babies happen all the time, all over the world. This certainly wasn't the first time this story had been written.

The next evening, I joined my friends for dinner at a restaurant featuring Western cuisine. Aside from the burgers and salads that most foreigners flocked to were also pitchers full of cocktails. You could order enough vodka and Redbull to satiate a small army, or enjoy a gallon of tequila sunrises all to yourself. In truth, this was the real reason we were there that night, as a pregame to the teacher weekend. But I wasn't drinking, and the group took notice. When I told them I was pregnant, rounds of congratulations exploded from the table. My Scottish friend cried tears of happiness, which greatly moved me, and I cried along with her.

Despite how easy it was for me to give up the alcohol, I had a terribly hard time quitting smoking. In fact, it felt like no matter how hard I tried, I just couldn't stop. I was smoking close to two packs per day before finding out I was pregnant, and although I had cut back my intake immediately, the cravings for just one more constantly enveloped my mind. Fortunately, an internet search told me that cessation by the fourth month should mitigate the worst of the risks that came with smoking while pregnant, so I afforded myself some grace in that department.

I didn't want to stop socializing, either. I followed my friends to the bars that night, sipping on juices, coffees, and specialty teas the establishments offered. Our favorite bartender was kind enough to make me his signature mocktail, and told me I should expect these for the next nine months. Still, I could tell by the looks in some of the eyes of our extended social circle that not everyone was excited, and there were no secrets in small, lazy Jinan. It wasn't long before everyone knew I was pregnant, and thankfully, everybody kept their opinions to themselves.

Breaking the news to my family was a bit like breaking the news to Samm. It happened over a group text between my parents, my siblings, and myself. They were all supportive, yet worried about my position. They treaded lightly while asking me if I was going to keep the baby, and my brother was particularly excited when I confirmed that I would. My brother had always been a fan of children, especially at the thought of having his own, although as of writing this, he hasn't been granted the opportunity. Being an uncle would be the next closest thing.

Now that my friends and family knew, the only person left to tell was Alimu. I waited two days for his call, and it didn't go as well as I'd hoped. The conversation with Alimu started off sweetly, with him taking great interest in everything I'd been doing since we last spoke and making promises about our future together. Bringing up the topic of the future felt like the best opportunity to tell him about our future family.

"Alimu," I began, "I really need to tell you something... and I think it will make you very happy."

"What is it?" he asked.

"I'm pregnant!" I giggled excitedly.

Alimu was silent for a moment, then shouted into the phone, "GET RID OF IT!"

I was so taken aback that I physically recoiled from the phone. Get rid of it? That was his first reaction? No joy, no happiness, not even any hint of surprise! Just anger. I had never experienced anger from Alimu before.

"We don't need a baby," he said sternly. "You have to have an abortion. There's no discussing this. Go tomorrow."

"I'm not going to have an abortion," I told him. "And I thought you'd be happy for us!"

"I am so unhappy, I'm the complete opposite of happy. How could you think this would make me happy?" he barked. Then continued, "I'm not going to talk to you again until you've had that abortion." Then he hung up the phone.

I cried for hours that night. I tried calling him back several times, but the phone just rang into the infinite darkness. I tried his siblings next. I told Qiong, Su'erdai, and Yonus that I was pregnant and that I wanted to keep the baby. They all congratulated me and asked me about their brother's reaction. When I told them about his response, they told me they would try to talk to him but couldn't guarantee that they could get him to change his mind. I thanked them for their willingness to help, as well as for their support towards me.

I felt so alone. The person I needed the most had rejected me, and now here I was in this great big country so far from home, essentially by myself. My friends could only help me so much, but they had their own lives to live, and I was about to diverge onto the path of becoming a full-fledged adult. Just then, as if he could sense my distress from across the ocean, my brother reached out to me. He asked me how I was doing and what I was thinking, and all of my emotions came tumbling out.

I told him about Alimu's reaction, about my friends' reactions, about the reactions of the peripheral foreigners in our groups, and I admitted that I was beginning to waver in my decision to keep the baby. How could this even be a good idea? I didn't even have a house for us to live in. I knew I could always go home, but at what cost? Life would essentially be over for me if I was going to do this alone. I didn't *want* to do this alone. What kind of a life would this baby have if it didn't have a father? On the other hand, people grow up without fathers all the time, and I wouldn't be *totally* alone. My family would be there to help me, but was now really the best time? Was I making an emotional decision instead of a logical one?

I tried to leave my emotional brain behind me and instead function with just the half of me that still held reason. My brother and I talked everything through. All the possibilities. What would life with a baby look like? What would it look like without a baby? What sacrifices would I be making for this baby? What sacrifices would I be making if I aborted it? Was I strong enough to go down either path? I chain-smoked and talked with my brother until the sun rose. We were both mentally exhausted from our conversation, but I had come to the ultimate decision that it was the most logical and responsible conclusion to terminate my pregnancy.

But I didn't know how to do that. I knew that abortions were legal in China for anyone that asked, and all I needed to do was ask, but I didn't want to go alone. I didn't even know the word for "abortion" in Chinese, and navigating the Chinese hospitals usually wasn't something we foreigners would tackle alone. Even those of us who spoke the best Chinese took a friend. Who could go with me that would be able to help? None of the friends who I would want with me for such an emotionally charged and controversial task could speak Chinese any better than I could. In fact, I was usually the one translating for them. So, I reached out to the only person who I thought would be both willing and able to help me through this journey: Zhen.

Zhen was remarried now, but he was willing to help. It was still too early in the morning to go to the hospital. The women's department didn't open until eight a.m., and Zhen and his wife were still getting out of bed. I felt bad for calling so early. But he told me to get ready and they'd meet me at the convenience store halfway between our two apartments in two hours. I didn't know Zhen's wife well, but in truth, I was thankful that she would be there with me. A woman would understand.

We took a bus together to the hospital. The line for the women's clinic was long, and we waited for close to two hours before being seen.

In China, there is no privacy in the hospitals. The waiting room was adjacent to three clinic rooms, each of which had open doors. Women lined up and peered into the rooms, anxiously awaiting their turn with the doctor. When it was my turn, there were no gowns to put on, and no curtains to hide behind when they asked to do a vaginal examination. Dozens of eyes peered at me, curious about what a foreigner was doing in this wing of the hospital. While laying on the bed, I heard one woman remark about the curly hair on my nethers, as opposed to her straight hair.

Zhen and his wife told the doctors what I wanted, but all they did was shake their heads.

"Based on the information she gave us about when her last period was, it's still too early to have an abortion. She has to be at least six weeks along before the pills will work effectively. She needs to wait another week," they said.

I tried to protest, tried to find a way for them to induce an abortion, asked Zhen if he could get the pills from somewhere else, begged for anything else other than waiting a week. I knew I wouldn't last a week. I knew that if I had to wait any longer with this baby growing inside of me, there would be no abortion. There would just be a baby. Zhen was very sorry, and he grabbed my shoulders trying to get me to calm down. His wife explained that they actually could get the pills without the doctors, but it would be very dangerous and might not work effectively. Then I'd have to go through all of this again, if not worse. She told me that all I needed to do was wait a week, and she'd come back to the hospital with me, and we could get the pills.

But a week later, I declined the offer to return to the hospital. I made my decision the moment I left the hospital grounds. I would keep the baby, and I would go home where my brother and my family could support me. My brother told me I could live with him, and he would help me raise it until I could get back on my feet. I was grateful for the offer, and I felt confident that the two of us could pull it off. My brother lived just a quarter mile from my parents, adjacent to their property, so it's not like we would be completely alone going into this. It was decided, then, I would go home. Except there was just one issue—I didn't have my passport!

Without a passport, it would be impossible to board a plane home. Claiming my passport had been stolen or lost would mean going to Beijing for a new one, as well as shelling out fines for replacing the visa. I didn't have my original invitation letters, and the University was on break now. I didn't even have the funds to make it to Beijing because I was throwing everything I was making back into Da Zhang's bank account. This was a problem, I thought to myself, that I can solve on my own. I didn't want to involve my parents or the police. I had gotten myself into this mess, so I could get myself out.

Alimu called me back three days later. He was incredibly angry that I hadn't had an abortion. I relayed to him the story of the hospital, and he berated me for not having the courage to wait another week. I told him that I intended to return home and have the baby by myself, that he didn't have to be involved if he didn't want to, but that I did need him to repay me as soon as possible. Alimu told me that he was already in the process of selling his lorry, and would give me back all fifty thousand yuan once he completed that task. He assured me that it wouldn't take much longer. I felt a sense of relief rush over me. With that money, I could not only get my passport back, but also afford rent and plane tickets home for both me and the cats. This certainly wasn't how I wanted things to go, but I couldn't force him into wanting this baby that I had now grown attached to.

Chapter 17

Two months later, Alimu and I were still at odds. I had paid Da Zhang back about twenty thousand yuan, but that was still less than half of what I needed to get my passport back. Furthermore, with the school still keeping me at part-time hours, I just didn't have the funding to stay in my apartment much longer. I knew I had at least until the end of the month, but then I would be out of luck. Alimu was supposed to be sending me money he'd made from selling his lorry in order to get my passport back, and I was just waiting until the month's end, planning on using a portion of it to pay rent and the other portion to give to Da Zhang.

But in truth, Alimu still hadn't sold his truck, and I'd received no money. I wasn't exactly flat broke, but I certainly didn't have enough funds for the next three months' worth of rent, and my landlord wouldn't accept a month-to-month lease. I was in a desperate situation and turned to both Muhaimai and Samm for help. Muhaimai helped me rent a small flatbed lorry, and a group of strong moving men helped me load up all of my non-essential belongings and transport them to ChangQing, where they were stored in his extra room above the noodle shop. Samm took in me. I had to move my cats in with a friend, as Samm was allergic, and her tiny loft apartment was no place for two zooming felines.

I came to her studio apartment with my big marital blanket and pillow, a duffel bag of clothes and miscellaneous belongings, my electronics, and my toiletries. "Home" was now at the foot of Samm's bed, my little space on the floor. What the hell was happening? This wasn't how anything was supposed to be! But at least I had a friend that loved me dearly and was going well out of her way to keep me from spiraling into despair. And as I lay in my makeshift bed that first night, falling into my phone, I knew I had to act fast if I didn't want to end up in any more trouble than I was already in.

I decided to talk to the manager of my English training school. They had already loaned me money once for a plane ticket, and I'd paid that back with no issues. This time, I would ask for a big enough loan to pay back DaZhang. Recently, he had been threatening to go to the police if he didn't get repaid soon. That was a mess I didn't want to be in. For someone technically living in the country illegally, the last thing I needed was attention from the police.

The English training school was about to send me on a trip to Hong Kong to renew my visa, which dictated that I needed to leave the country once every 90 days in order for the visa to remain valid. Mine was set to expire in a week. The Hong Kong runs were always stressful—I had to first travel to the major costal city of ShenZhen then cross over through border patrol into Hong Kong. Once in Hong Kong, I had to take a series of subways into the city proper, only to turn around and go right back out the same way I came in. There was lots of waiting in line, lots of shuffling around, and it made for a long day.

May, the school manager, told me that the school couldn't loan me any more money. The owner hadn't liked that they gave me money for a plane ticket home over the summer, even though the funds were paid back with my monthly salary. Still, May told me that she trusted me, so would give me a personal loan from her own bank account. I told her about Alimu's plan to sell his lorry and send me the funds, and that I would pay her back as soon as that money came through. May knew that I had a Chinese boyfriend, but she didn't know I was pregnant, or that things between Alimu and I had taken a turn for the worse. I didn't tell her, though. I wasn't sure just how much I wanted my boss to know about my private life, even if she was doing me a kindness. She certainly wasn't impressed when I told her that Alimu was Hui and living in Qinghai.

But May handed over 30,000 yuan and wished me luck on my journey to Hong Kong. I immediately called Da Zhang.

"I have the money," I said, "I can give it to you now."

"I'm not in town right now," he responded, "but I have a friend who can handle the exchange. Meet him at the train station at eight p.m. tonight."

Great, I thought to myself, things just keep getting more complicated. However, I needed to leave as soon as possible for ShenZhen, and plane ticket prices were jumping by the day. I waited until that evening, then headed out to the train station. I called Da Zhang when I got there.

"I'm here," I said. "Where's your friend?"

"He'll be there soon," Da Zhang said. "Just find a spot and wait."

I cleared the dust away from a section of high steps in front of a now-closed convenience store, between a McDonald's and a cigarette shop, and sat down. An hour passed, but I still hadn't heard from Da Zhang or his friend. I called Da Zhang again.

"I've been here for an hour, is your friend going to be here soon?" I asked.

"My friend says he's there and can't find you! Are you tricking us?" Da Zhang snapped at me.

It took several moments before we realized that while I was waiting at the central railway station for slow-speed trains, Da Zhang's friend had traveled to the far side of the city to wait at the high-speed railway station. And it was another hour still before he made his way to my location.

The man who approached me was of a smaller frame, with hair that fell just above his ears and thick, black glasses.

"Hello! Are you Anna?" he asked me sheepishly.

"I am. Are you Da Zhang's friend?" I asked in return.

He nodded. "Da Zhang told me that I need to count all the money before I give you back your passport."

"Of course," I agreed but secretly thumbed away a one-hundred-yuan bill back into my purse. I'm still not clear on what my motivation was, other than I was feeling stressed and angry, and wanted to see if he would make a fuss over a hundred yuan. He counted the money slowly, in front of the entire crowd. Although there weren't many people around since it was so late at night, trains would come and go at all hours of the day, so we were far from the only two there. At last, he finished.

"You're missing a hundred yuan," he said, and stared at me blankly.

"Oh, sorry," I replied simply, and retrieved the last bill from my purse.

Once I handed it over, Da Zhang's friend reached inside his coat for my passport.

"And this belongs to you!" he chirped happily. But as I reached for it, he pulled his hand back a little and continued, "It really is a cool passport, I was looking through all the neat photos on the way over here and—"

"Thanks," I snapped, more hastily than intended, and grabbed my passport out of his hands.

"Well, I guess that's all! It was great to meet you!" Da Zhang's friend said cheerily, then walked off into the night.

I finally had my passport back! Relief was seeping through my pores as I slid the little booklet into my purse. The weight those few pages felt like a thousand pounds, and for a moment I found it hard to catch my breath. Still, my work for the night wasn't over. I had to buy plane tickets and get my ass to Hong Kong! I had enough money in my personal savings for a plane ticket, a hotel, and food without breaking the bank, so the first thing I did on the taxi ride back to Samm's was book my tickets to ShenZhen. Flying to Hong Kong directly counted as an international flight, meaning prices were extreme. However, flying to ShenZhen and crossing the border on foot was much cheaper. Just slightly more complicated.

The next thing I did was call Alimu. I told him I got my passport back, but I'd taken out a loan from my manager to do so. I still needed to pay her back, and I still needed money for plane tickets home. I didn't have to worry about rent anymore, which meant fewer expenses, but I would eventually need to find a place to live that wasn't Samm's floor. I didn't plan on being in China for much longer, but I needed to at least work long enough to either pay back May or pay for my international flight tickets home. I could do it in a month or two if I played my cards right, meaning I could tie up all my loose ends in China and still be home in the US before the baby came, but the ball had to get rolling, and now. I stressed this urgency to Alimu, and he told me that he was actively in the process of completing the sale of his lorry. He would have the funds in two or three days.

Next, I texted Yonus. Surprisingly, Yonus and I had developed quite the friendship over the past two months. Yonus was kind and gentle with a calm demeanor that greatly resembled his brother. He gave me a lot of insight into Alimu and explained that growing up, Alimu's household was far from happy. His stepfather regularly beat him, his siblings, and his mother. The violence in the house was astounding, and sometimes punishment for the children meant watching their mother be abused. Yonus was lucky to have escaped all of that, growing up with his uncle's family instead. Yonus had been married once, but it was an arranged marriage, and his wife didn't really love him. After they had a son together, she fell in love with someone else and divorced Yonus, leaving their son behind, too.

At one point, Yonus and I were seriously considering trying to make a life together. He wanted his son to grow up in a happy home with a mother who loved him like her own (which was a rarity in China—stepchildren are generally not treated as well as biological children), with siblings and parents who didn't have to work too hard and who could be home for dinner every night. He wanted to run away from his life in Qinghai. It was taking him nowhere. He wasn't happy, and the world was big. He could be my baby's father, he'd suggested. We wouldn't have to worry about Alimu because we would never see

Alimu. He wanted to cut out Alimu from his life completely after seeing the way he was treating me. Yonus had trade skills that would allow him to get a job anywhere, and we fantasized about running off to different places around China—Yunnan, Tibet, Guilin, all the beautiful places—and several countries outside of China, too.

We had gotten swept up in our fantasies. Still, families could be formed under the strangest of circumstances, and historically marriage for love was a new concept in our timeline. He and I could at least try together, right? We both had the same goal. When things started getting serious, Yonus started talking about asking his father for permission to be with me. I told Yonus he was a twenty-five-year-old man, he didn't need anybody's permission to do anything. But he insisted that he needed his father's blessing before pursuing a possible marriage and needed to know that his family would be there to support him in his decisions. He was fine with never seeing Alimu again, but couldn't stand the thought of never seeing his father—his uncle—again. Unfortunately, Yonus's father forbade him from starting a life with me, threatening to cut him off forever if we decided to tread that path. I suppose marrying your older brother's lover wasn't exactly the future Yonus's father wanted for him. We both felt dejected, and Yonus wept. He stopped reaching out as much after that, and slowly our everyday conversations became once-a-week conversations.

I wasn't too sad about Yonus, and I wasn't mad at him. We tried with our flights of fancy, and it didn't work. I was disappointed that our plan to run off and make a life together wasn't going to pan out, but it wasn't like I loved Yonus. I was certainly thankful for his care, but we owed each other nothing. So, when I texted Yonus about Alimu's promise to repay, it was to confirm that he was, in fact, in the process of selling his lorry. Yonus confirmed that what Alimu was saying was true, and that I could expect repayment from him before I reached ShenZhen. Yonus said he would make sure I got everything I was owed, and I was grateful.

Chapter 18

The flight to ShenZhen was uneventful. Arriving in the late afternoon, the air in southern China was hot and humid. We were close to the ocean, and despite the onset of fall in Jinan, the trees here were still green and the water was still warm. Locals dressed in loose-fitting clothes, mostly shorts and sandals. The women wore dresses that barely covered their thighs, and the men took their shirts off completely. The breeze, when it could be found, carried the scent of salt water and garbage through the city of twelve million people.

I took a black cab from the airport to the border crossing. A "black cab" referred to any vehicle used as a taxi that wasn't registered as a taxi. Black cabs were usually fancier cars that allowed for comfortable travel, especially when taxis were hard to find, but they were also more expensive. My black cab driver had a more than fair price, though, because he still needed to drop someone else off and pick someone else up, and I would be his in-between stop. It meant that I wouldn't be on a direct path to Hong Kong, but I wasn't exactly in a hurry.

An hour later, I was at the border crossing between ShenZhen and Hong Kong. I held my breath as the border guards eyed my passport, then me, then my visa, then me again, before finally placing their exit stamp in the back of the book. I let out a sigh of relief as I made my way to the adjoining subway station. Getting out was half the battle, now the only thing left was to get back in. I rode the subway through its first stop, then got out and changed platforms to ride the line the same way back. The pregnancy was making me feel nauseous, and the gentle rocking of the subway wasn't helping. However, I managed to hold it together long enough to make it out of the subway before vomiting all over a nearby bathroom floor.

Next came the long process of waiting in line for re-entry. I stared for a long time at the signs placed throughout the crossing hall that limited the transportation of baby formula to two cans per person. These were the remnants of the 2008 Chinese Milk Scandal, when thousands flocked to Hong Kong in an attempt to find safe formula after a safety recall in the mainland. Bodies pressed against bodies in the re-entry line. Everyone from babies to the elderly was drenched in sweat, as the crossing hall didn't have strong enough air conditioning to combat the evening humidity. After an hour and a half of waiting, a border guard pressed his big red stamp into the back of my passport and once more I entered mainland China.

It was getting late now, nearing eight p.m., and I was ready for the day to be over. My feet hurt, my uterus hurt, and I was both exhausted and starving. I hailed a cab to take me to the hotel that I booked in advance, hoping the hotel's AC would be able to cool the whole room. But when I approached the front desk to check in, the receptionist gave me some terrible news. Since I was so late, they had given my room to someone else!

"But it's not even nine o'clock yet! How can you say I'm late?" I protested.

"The hotel's check-in time starts at two p.m. You selected your check-in time as six p.m. when you booked with us. It's now well after six p.m., and there were other guests who were waiting for your room," said the receptionist robotically.

I was bewildered. Nothing like this had ever happened before. Sure, I'd heard of hotels giving away rooms if you hadn't shown up by midnight, but this was a first.

"But I paid for the room in advance! See, here's my receipt!" I pulled out my phone to show the woman my confirmation.

"But you're late," she said coldly.

"Fine," I said, "I'll take whatever room you have left then," and I said goodbye to my dream of a big, comfy queen bed.

"No, you don't understand," said the receptionist. "We're full. Completely booked. There are no more rooms. That's why we gave yours away."

I was so mad that I began to cry, "Well, then I need my money back!"

"We can't give you your money back," she said to me harshly, "because it's not our fault you were late!"

"Well then you had better call the police," I said firmly, "because I'm NOT leaving!"

And with that, I picked up my belongings and sat down in the only lobby chair, crossing my arms and grumbling to myself. The receptionist walked over to me and asked me to leave. Her face was expressionless. I told her again that I wasn't leaving, that if she wanted me to leave, it would have to be the police that made me go. I didn't care if I was being illogical. I felt wronged, and I couldn't go trekking around the city to find a new hotel that would take foreigners. At this point, I couldn't even afford a new hotel!

It only took about fifteen minutes before a police officer came through the hotel doors. He spoke with the receptionist, who pointed him in my direction. He stood over me, placed his hands on his hips, and asked me what was going on. I explained to him that I had just come back from Hong Kong, had purchased this room in advance, and now I was being told that not only could I not stay here, but that I couldn't get my money back either. I told the officer that I was pregnant, exhausted, and hadn't eaten all day, that all I wanted to do was find somewhere to sleep before boarding the hellish slow train back to Jinan, which was going to be a two-day journey on a hard seat. I couldn't afford a round-trip plane ticket, but train tickets were much cheaper.

The police officer's face and body language softened, and he told me to wait a moment. Then he turned around and walked out. He returned moments after, asking me how much I had paid for my hotel room, before silently leaving again. When he came back a half-hour later, he told the receptionist to refund my money. She complied. Then he led me down two blocks and across the street to a nearby *zhaodaisuo*, a type of hotel and entertainment club that was generally off-limits to foreigners. This *zhaodaisuo* offered massages, computers, and karaoke, and posters shouting out the dangers of street drugs lined the walls. As the police officer and I walked up the steps to the reception area, I saw a group of very pretty, very scantily clad women scamper off from the lobby to their respective rooms. Prostitutes often turned to a *zhaodaisuo* to practice their trade, giving the owner a percentage of their nightly earnings.

"You can stay here. They already have a room set up for you," the police officer told me, "But you'll need to pay the same fee that you paid in the other hotel. Just take the money you got back and pay the owner here. After tonight, negotiations are up to you." He smiled at me and wished me luck as he turned to leave. I thanked him profusely for his help. He waved his hand at me and said, "It's my job to help."

The receptionist of the *zhaodaisuo* was also the owner, and he greeted me warmly with a smile that spread across his entire face.

"Thank you for taking me in tonight," I told him.

"Awww, it's no big deal! We're happy to have you! Just wait until I tell grandpa that I have a pregnant foreigner in MY hotel!" he spoke delightedly.

Then a woman appeared from behind a curtain that hung over the door behind the reception desk. "Come with me," she said. "I'll show you your room."

I followed her down a series of hallways until we came to a small room towards the back of the building. Inside was enough space for two single beds and a nightstand. The beds were pressed against the walls on either side, leaving just a narrow space to walk between them. There was a bathroom, raised up from the rest of the room, which took up more than a quarter of the room's space. Inside was a squatty potty toilet and a shower, but at least the shower head wasn't directly over the toilet. Instead, it was off to the side. That was a nice little feature.

The room wasn't much, but it would do in a pinch. I wasn't planning to stay there long. All I needed to do was book my train tickets. Alimu had told me the day before that the money from selling his truck would hit my account that day. I thanked the woman for taking me to my room. She nodded, smiled, then walked away. I threw my backpack on one bed, then flopped face down onto the other. It felt divine to no longer be in an upright position, but I couldn't rest too long. Those tickets wouldn't buy themselves.

Upon checking my bank account, I found that no money had been transferred to me. Waves of anger swept through my body. He had promised! And this was for something important! I immediately tried to call Alimu but got no answer. I tried calling Yonus, but there was no answer from him either. It certainly wasn't too late in the evening to be calling. These men were night owls. I tried texting instead. Alimu wasn't even online, so I didn't expect to hear from him any time soon, but Yonus was listed as active. I confronted him about the money, asking if he knew anything about Alimu. Yonus responded that Alimu had already sold the lorry and was supposed to give me the money today. He wasn't sure why he hadn't. He offered to call Alimu for me, and I took him up on the offer.

Yonus texted again a short time later. He told me that he'd spoken with Alimu, and that Alimu agreed to pay me in the morning when he could get to the nearest bank. He couldn't do anything right now because all the banks were closed, and it was too large an amount of money to transfer directly through the ATM system. I sighed reluctantly, but there wasn't much I could do about the situation, at least not tonight. I decided the best thing to do in that moment would be to find sleep, but sleep did not want to be found. Instead, I tossed and turned for hours before giving up and opening my laptop, resuming the binge watching of my latest tv show.

I woke up the next morning with a dead laptop. I had fallen asleep at some point, although I didn't know when. I didn't even know the time upon waking. My phone was dead, too, and there were no clocks in the room. With no windows, it felt like time was standing still. The whole world was just me and that little room. I sighed deeply, plugged in my electronics to charge, and made my way to the bathroom for a shower. I didn't need to wait long for the water to warm up, which was a relief, and it stayed warm for the entirety of my shower, another kindness from the universe.

After getting dressed, I checked my phone. It was ten-thirty a.m. I could have slept longer if I wanted, as I had nowhere to be and nothing to do except wait for Alimu. I couldn't get back to Jinan without being paid back, and if I were going to be in ShenZhen for more than a day, I really needed to conserve my money. The last thing I needed was to be stranded in a major city with no way home, and I was now facing the possibility of that very situation becoming my reality. I turned on my still-charging phone and called Alimu. He answered.

"I'll have your money to you today," he said. "I just have to get to the bank. Give me a few hours."

"I really can't wait much longer, you know. I really need to go home," I said.

Alimu's voice softened, "I know. I'm working as hard as I can on this. Just be patient, okay?"

What else could I do but wait? My stomach growled at me like a mad dog, and I knew I had to at least get out of that room and find something to eat. Luckily, right next to the *zhaodaisuo* was a small convenience store, run out of a garage next to a tire shop. There wasn't much there, but I could pick up water, drinks, and some cheap instant noodles. I bought enough food to get me through the night but was reluctant to buy too much, lest I'd need to leave it behind to travel. Before I could head back inside, the most intoxicating smell drifted by. It smelled so familiar, and foreign, like it was coming from a three-star Italian restaurant.

I walked out onto the sidewalk and tried to follow my nose. Where was that smell coming from? It smelled so delicious! Whatever it was, I needed it. I traced the scent across the street, coming from an independent noodle shop. I walked inside. The scent of meat and tomato sauce and cheese filled my nostrils. And there, up on the menu board, plastered on a bright red background, was the picture of a piece of lasagna. I had to have it. I NEEDED it. Never in a hundred years had I expected to end up on a random street in ShenZhen buying lasagna from a completely random noodle house, but there I was. It was as if the stars had aligned, and the heavens were raining down manna in the form of cheese and carbs. I hurriedly counted out eighteen yuan and bought a slice. Piping hot, I carried the lasagna and my bag of drinks and snacks back up to my hotel room. I sat down on the bed and experienced a brief moment of panic before realizing that the lasagna had indeed come with its own fork. Tucking into the pasta dish, tears rolled down my cheeks. This was the highest elevation of comfort food, and I desperately needed to be comforted.

I spent the rest of the day locked away in my windowless hotel room, binge watching tv shows on my laptop. I didn't want to go outside. The air was humid enough to slice through, and the temperatures were high well into the evening. If I wasn't in direct air conditioning, I would sweat profusely. Jinan was never this hot. My hometown was never this hot. I questioned how so many human beings could live in a place so terribly muggy, and I waited for Alimu's money.

Around four o'clock, I tried calling him again. He declined the call, so I texted him. He never responded. I got nothing but radio silence from Yonus, too. I didn't want to bother him too much since he wasn't his brother's keeper, but he was the closest connection that I had to Alimu, and I was beginning to feel desperate. I was checking my bank account every fifteen minutes, and I was an emotional wreck. I was blaming myself for not being patient enough to wait for Alimu, not just on that day, but throughout our whole relationship. If I hadn't been so impatient, he could have bought that lorry on his own instead of needing me to fund it. If I hadn't been so impatient, he would have saved up enough money to move to Jinan, instead of me tracking him down with his siblings in Qilian. If I had only been more patient with him then, maybe things would be different now.

A major part of me also wondered if I shouldn't be more patient with Alimu on the subject of the baby. After all, we are often told that women become mothers when they are pregnant while men don't become fathers until their child is born. Maybe Alimu just needed more time to process. That happened all the time. I could find countless stories online about women whose boyfriends initially asked for an abortion, then changed their minds immediately upon seeing their baby for the first time, sometimes even sooner, and everybody was living as one happy family. Maybe I just needed to be more patient again. Could I give him that grace? My heart felt so conflicted, and I had a bad habit of blaming myself for everything that had gone wrong. This time, I was more than halfway convinced that everything that had gone wrong in our relationship was due to my impatience.

As night fell on ShenZhen, my bank account remained empty and Alimu remained offline. Furthermore, his phone was either off or dead. Anger, fear, and anxiety began to roil up in me again but was interrupted by a knock at the door. It was the owner's wife, and she'd brought me supper. Fried green beans and beef on rice, nothing special, but a dish she'd cooked in her home just for me. "For the baby," she said, and smiled at me. I tried not to grab at the bowl too greedily as I accepted her offer of food. I had a hard time staying full lately, and her cooking smelled wonderful. It tasted even better than I imagined, and I finished every morsel of what was in that bowl. I was touched by her kindness towards strangers.

The second and third days passed the same as the first, minus the lasagna. I was at the point where I couldn't wait around for Alimu anymore. Something had to be done. I had been talking with my karaoke group about my situation, as they were a welcome distraction to the darkness of the windowless room. They knew all about Alimu, our relationship, the baby, the decline of our relationship, and now that Alimu was withholding money from me. This angered our group leader, YouLai, who took great pride in both his culture and religion. YouLai told me that what Alimu was doing was both an abomination to Hui men across China and Muslim men across the world, and that if I could get out to Xining, he would make sure that I got paid back. He told me that it would be easy to find Alimu, especially if his brother was working in Xining, and that there was no way Alimu would ignore him. It was a matter of principle.

I felt uncertain if going back to Xining would be worth the time and effort, but YouLai was insistent, and fifty thousand yuan was on the line. This was no small beans. Maybe going to Xining and trusting in YouLai was the right choice to make, but I still didn't have the money it would take to get out there. There were no train tickets left that weren't standing-room only, and I didn't want to have to stand for the thirty-five-hour-long journey. This was before bullet trains between the cities were available, so the only trains were agonizingly slow. Searching online, the cheapest plane ticket from ShenZhen to Xining cost a little less than two thousand yuan. It wasn't an exorbitant amount, but I couldn't sacrifice the money I had left.

I wasn't without a stroke of luck, however. Throughout the past few days, I had been keeping in contact with a close friend from Pakistan, Khan. Khan was studying to be a doctor in Jinan and was concerned about my situation. He, too, was angry that a Muslim man was acting this way, especially towards a woman. He constantly checked in on me, worried that I was alone and struggling. When I told him about YouLai's plan, he offered to pay for the plane ticket. He told me that I would be on my own for getting back to Jinan, but at least he could help in some manner. I promised to repay him as soon as Alimu gave me the money and thanked him for his generosity. Then I booked a plane ticket for the following morning, packed my belongings, and settled my tab with the *zhaodaisuo*.

Chapter 19

It was mid-morning when YouLai picked me up from the airport in Xining. He had a friend with him, another member of our singing group that rarely participated but was still well known. As we drove from the airport to the city, YouLai ran through the list of members in our group and where in the city, or near the city, they all lived. YouLai was shorter than the average man, but extremely lean and muscular. Working out and showing off his progress was a passion for him, and he engaged in as many types of martial arts as he could study. He had a long face and hair that was styled short, but not too short that it couldn't come to a point in the front, as if the wild mountain air was blowing at him from behind, streamlining his hair in the wind.

As we approached the city, YouLai started asking more questions about Alimu. He asked to see the photo of his license and any other photos I had of him, but he told me nothing of his actual plans. Nearing the center of the city, YouLai suddenly pulled into the parking lot of a large hotel. He told me to wait in the car while he went inside. His friend left with him, and while YouLai was inside the hotel, his friend greeted two other men that had pulled up across from us. I didn't recognize these men, either, but one of them playfully grabbed at YouLai when he finally came back outside.

"Okay, I need Alimu's phone number now," he told me as he opened my car door.

"I'll give it to you, but he hasn't been answering me, even when I've tried on someone else's phone," I told him. I had tried twice in ShenZhen to use the owner's phone to call him, but both times were unsuccessful.

"Oh, he'll answer my call," YouLai stated confidently. I didn't know how he could be so sure of himself.

As soon as YouLai pressed the dial button on his cell phone, Alimu answered his phone. I'm not sure what the two of them spoke about since they were speaking in *Qinghai Hua*, but I assumed he was either threatened by YouLai or lured to the hotel by the promise of a business transaction. Either way, the phone call lasted for less than five minutes, and after YouLai was finished, the four men ushered me upstairs to the just-booked hotel room to wait for Alimu. While we waited, YouLai asked me to tell him everything that was going on between Alimu and I, all from the beginning. I told him everything I could but didn't have much time before there was a knock at the door. It was Alimu!

YouLai opened the door, and he walked in slowly, looking around at all four men before landing his eyes on me. He started to walk towards me, but YouLai stopped him. The men all gathered around Alimu, forming a circle in the middle of the hotel room. They spoke in slow, cool, and even tones. Nobody sounded upset, anxious, or angry. Nobody sounded worried. Nobody raised their voice, nor quickened their pace. Occasionally, they would look in my direction or YouLai would subconsciously point a finger my way.

After a few minutes, their conversation was over, and the three strange men left the hotel room leaving only myself, YouLai, and Alimu.

"We're going to give you two some time alone," YouLai told me. Then he turned and left the room.

Alimu let out a deep sigh and turned to me. "What are you doing here, Anna?" he asked.

"I need my money, Alimu," I responded. "That's why I'm here."

"But you already have your passport back, don't you?" Alimu questioned. "So what's the big rush?"

"I need the money to get home," I explained. "International plane tickets are expensive, and now I have debts to repay. I can't go home without this money."

"Here," he said, and reached into his bag, pulling out a wad of money. "Here's five thousand yuan. It's all I have right now. I gave the money from the lorry to Yonus so he could transfer it to you yesterday. I don't know why he didn't, but I'll find out."

"Why didn't you just transfer the money directly to me? Why did you have to give it to Yonus?" I asked.

"Because Yonus can do it easier than I can. He's here in town, and I was out of town," he reasoned. Then he grabbed my hand.

"Anna, I've really missed you…" he began, and grabbed my other wrist. Then he continued, "You know I never wanted us to end up like this. You just need to be more patient… even now, I still can't help but love you."

Then he pulled me close to him and kissed me. I kissed back. I considered resisting, but I was still in love with Alimu, and I wanted desperately for him to love me enough to love the baby, too. I had already decided I could forgive him, chalk it up to jitters and anxiety that stemmed around the cultural faux pas of having a baby out of wedlock. If we really did love each other, we could overcome anything. If I could just give him patience and grace, we could get through this and transform into the vision of the happy family that lived in my head. Alimu guided me to the bed and began to put his hands on my body. But just as he began to reach for his belt buckle, he was interrupted by a knock at the door.

We both jumped up, and I shuffled my clothes back around to keep what we'd been doing from becoming too obvious. When I opened the door, I not only saw YouLai and his three friends, but four other additional men had joined him. Big men. Tall men. Strong men. YouLai motioned for me to exit the hotel room, and I complied. All eight men piled into room, and I saw them circling Alimu before YouLai closed the door. Time passed. Five minutes. Ten minutes. Fifteen minutes. Finally, the door opened again and out stepped Alimu, eyes wide and hands trembling.

"I'll call you once I talk to Yonus," he said in a low voice before quickly making his way out of the hotel. YouLai stepped out of the room and into the hallway with me.

"You know, we were going to beat him up," he said as he handed me a cigarette, "but when you opened the door and I saw the look on your face, I knew we couldn't do that."

I wasn't shocked at the news that they had intended violence against him, but I didn't know what to say. I said nothing, and YouLai continued, "which is too bad, because I *really* wanted to hit him." Then he laughed and called back into the room for his friends. They poured out of the room into the hallway, shaking my hand and grinning at me as they passed by. Before I could say anything to them, my phone rang. It was Salihan.

Salihan told me that Alimu told him I was in Xining, and that I needed a place to stay until I got my money back. He told me that he would take me to a hotel that his friend's father owned. It was close to where Yonus worked, and the price was much less expensive than the usual chain hotels. Salihan texted me the address, and I showed it to YouLai. Luckily, it wasn't too far away, and YouLai said he could drive me there.

"I guess you'll just have to wait a couple days until he gets you the money," YouLai said as we pulled onto the road, "but he did make a promise to us that he'll pay you back. Unfortunately, I don't think we'll be able to get him to agree to meet with us again. We scared him pretty badly, but that should be a good thing for you!"

"I hope you're right," I said, "I can't stick around here forever, and if Alimu doesn't come through, I'm going to be stuck."

"I wish I could help more," said YouLai, "but I'm needed in Xi'An for business, or else I'd stay until you got the money back. If he backs out, text me again and I'll see what I can do."

YouLai stopped the car at a women's hospital and pointed across the street.

"Your hotel should be there. This is a pretty nice part of town, so no one should bother you here," he said reassuringly.

As we said our goodbyes, I saw Salihan walk up the street towards the hotel, and I crossed the road to meet him. Salihan was all smiles.

"It's good to see you again, Anna!" he shouted to me above the bustle of traffic.

"It's good to see you, too, Salihan," I said, "although I wish it were under better circumstances." I was still wary of Salihan. Alimu's whole family had all told me that Salihan could be "like a snake", and that he constantly told lies, but it also a relief to see Salihan. I knew that he was very close to Yonus, which meant that he was close to the person who had my money. Seeing him made me feel confident that everything would get sorted out. By now, it was likely that Alimu's entire family knew about the money I was owed, meaning the pressure would be on for him to return it in a timely fashion, lest the situation become more complicated than it already was.

Salihan led me inside the hotel and introduced me to the receptionist. "I come here all the time just to talk and relax," he said, and both he and the receptionist laughed. I paid for my room and followed Salihan up the stairs. I was out of breath by the time we reached the top, struggling to fill my lungs with the thin air. Although not as bad as Qilian, Xining was still well over 7,000 ft in elevation, and my pregnancy made me feel even more tired. I had to stop and concentrate on breathing deeply and slowing my heart rate to keep from hyperventilating. Salihan followed me into the hotel room, then handed me a cigarette from his pack.

"You really should stop smoking," he said. "It's bad for the baby."

"I know," I responded, "I'm trying… it's just been a struggle."

We smoked in silence, then Salihan stood up to leave. "I have to get back to work now," he said, "but if you need anything, I'll be online afterwards." With that, he left, leaving me alone in a Xining hotel room, surrounded by strangers, essentially broke, unsure of how any part of the near future would play out. I missed Jinan. I missed my friends and my cats, and I missed my family most of all, but there was nothing I could do now except continue to wait and hope. It was hope that I clung to for survival.

Chapter 20

The next day, Alimu texted me.

"Did Yonus give you the money yet?" his message read.

"No, I haven't heard anything from him," I responded.

"Okay, well you should call him if you haven't heard from him in a day. I'll call him, too" he texted.

I heard nothing else from anyone in Alimu's family that day, including his family in YangLong. That night, I wrote a long letter to Yonus, discussing not only how important this money was for me, but also his role in the baby's life, if he wanted a role as uncle, and the best way to keep in contact with him. Surprisingly, Salihan stopped by that night after work with dinner in tow, and I gave him the letter to hand to Yonus. He agreed to pass it along and stayed only long enough to smoke a cigarette before leaving for the night.

The next morning, I tried to call Yonus before his working hours but was unsuccessful in reaching him. So, I texted Salihan.

"Oh, Yonus left! He's gone off to a neighboring town for a construction job. He's driving a dump truck," Salihan texted back.

"Do you know how long he'll be gone? Did you give him the letter?"

"I don't know how long he'll be gone. Probably around a week," Salihan's message read.

"What about the letter," I pressed.

"He read it," he said, "then he ripped it up and threw it in the trash."

Ripped it up and threw it in the trash? That's such a strong reaction! I wouldn't have expected Yonus to behave that way. He had always kept a level head about things. Sure, if he didn't want to be in the baby's life, that's fine, but to rip up the letter then run away with my money? That wasn't okay. I immediately reached out to YouLai publicly in our karaoke group.

But before YouLai could respond, someone else spoke up.

"That town is only a couple of hours away. If you can pay for gas, I can drive you out there," read the message from JunGe.

Then YouLai responded, "You should go with JunGe. Finding this guy is going to be your best bet for getting your money back."

I messaged JunGe privately. "I can pay for gas. When can you leave?"

"Let's leave this evening. I'm busy until six o'clock," he said. "Ee can get a hotel for overnight, then start looking for him in the morning."

So that became the plan. A few hours later, I was in JunGe's car and we were headed east, possibly southeast. The name of the town Yonus was in has escaped my memory, and even after pouring over terrain maps of China, I can't seem to pinpoint exactly where it was. We drove for hours through canyons and cliffs carved out specifically for the roads, following the hills up and down as the red dirt from the rocks blew across the road. Dusk fell as we reached the base of a winding switchback road, and by the time we reached the top, it was full dark. The buildings of the city below, nestled between a bed of mountains, twinkled like stars and reflected on the still waters of a river flowing near the city. We headed down the mountain and into the valley of the city, the constant zigzagging motion rocking me like a slow ocean.

I wasn't expecting JunGe to pay for our accommodations, but to my surprise, he booked us two separate rooms in a cheap hotel on his own dime. When I insisted on paying him back, he told me that I could pay for dinner, but all the nearby restaurants were closed. This was such a small city that everything stopped after eight p.m., and all that was left open was a chain convenience store. We purchased a couple bowls of instant noodles and some jarred fruits for our dinners that night and retreated to our rooms. JunGe lingered in my room for a moment, and I felt the air around him tense. Was it sexual? But the moment passed, and he wished me goodnight before closing the door.

The hotel room was warm, thanks to the gas radiator that sat under the window. I stripped off my clothes and sat naked on the bed, flipping through the tv stations for something that might be in English. Finding nothing, I settled on a show about the Monkey King, a favorite topic in China adored by adults and children alike. I tried calling Yonus, but had no luck. Texting Salihan yielded better results. Salihan confirmed that he was sure Yonus and I were now in the same town, which made me feel better. Being in such a small place should make it easier to find him. How many construction sites could be in one town?

That question was answered easily the next morning. Aside from the construction happening right outside the hotel, a factory was being built on the outskirts of town. Dump trucks were hauling dirt to the property from another site that was on the way. We confirmed this information while speaking with a few other locals over a breakfast of steamed potato baozi and bowls of beef broth. Such a hearty meal was welcomed, and we both wolfed it down quickly before heading to his vehicle. As soon as JunGe and I got in the car, we saw a dump truck go by.

"Should we follow it?" I asked, "It could take us right where we need to be!"

"I was thinking the exact same thing," JunGe said.

He followed closely, but the dump truck was faster than we were, and traffic kept merging between us, pushing us farther and farther from the dump truck. It turned off on a dirt road, kicking up red dust in its wake, and we followed it until we came to a huge pit, easily a hundred feet across. Massive yellow backhoes were busy filling the beds of waiting trucks. This was obviously the source of the dirt being taken to the factory. But the road around the pit was rugged, with muddy trenches easily a foot deep, making our passage impossible.

"I don't think I can get through this, Anna," JunGe said apologetically. "My car just isn't built for this terrain."

"That's okay, JunGe," I said. "We were just testing our luck following this dump truck anyway. Why don't we go back to the main road and wait for a truck to leave? We can follow it to the factory."

JumGe agreed and we soon found the factory easily enough. But the entrance was guarded by a security booth with two men inside. I explained who we were and why we were there, then I showed them a photo of Yonus. One guard shook his head, but the other said he remembered seeing Yonus coming and going that morning. I asked if we could go inside and find him, but they said it wasn't allowed. But they said we were more than welcome to wait for Yonus as long as we stayed outside the gates.

JunGe asked me what I wanted to do. He said he had some errands to attend to, but if I wanted to wait for Yonus at the gates, he would pick me later and take me to lunch. I decided to wait at the gates and watch for Yonus. JunGe left me under the shade of a small row of poplar trees that lined the construction site's blue metal fence, and I positioned myself in a place that allowed me to clearly see the driver of any dump truck that made its way by.

For the next three hours, I waited on the side of the road. The dump trucks had to come to a complete stop before entering or leaving the factory property, so I saw the faces of every driver. At first there were ten trucks, then twenty, then thirty that passed either in or out of the site. None of them were Yonus. Had I missed him? Was this the wrong construction site? JunGe picked me up exactly when he said he would, and as we left to find lunch, I called Alimu. I wasn't expecting him to answer, but he picked up on the fifth ring.

"Hey Alimu. I'm trying to find Yonus. Salihan told me where to go, but he's not here," I said.

"Salihan is a God-damned liar, Anna" Alimu said calmly. "Yonus isn't there. He's still in Xining. He never left."

"Well, he's not answering my phone calls!" I cried. "And I'm tired of chasing everybody around just to get paid back!"

"It's between you and him now," Alimu said. "I'm not responsible for this anymore. I gave the money to Yonus. He's the one responsible. I'll call him again. Come back to Xining." He hung up before I could say anything else.

"What do you want to do now?" JunGe asked.

"What else can we do besides go back to Xining?" I said, my voice trailing off slowly.

I was drained. Mentally extinguished. I felt like I was on a never-ending wild goose chase for people who were going out of their way to ignore me, and I needed to come to terms with the fact that I was probably never going to see that money again.

I spent the entirety of the car ride mulling over what to do. What exactly were my options? I could always call my parents and ask them to rescue me, but that was an absolute last resort and the one thing above all that I didn't want to happen. I could go back to Xining and get the police involved, but then they'd probably find out that I was working in China illegally and I'd have even bigger problems. I could go back to Jinan, but where would I stay? I couldn't just live on Samm's floor forever, and I needed a new job with better hours. The last option was doable, but how long would it take to accomplish? Could I even make enough money on my own before it was time to go back to the States? I was on a time limit after all.

We eventually made it back to Xining, and JunGe dropped me back off at the hotel. The only thing I could think to do was lie on the bed and try to breathe. I was mad at Salihan. I was mad at Yonus. And I was mad at Alimu. What was with this family? I had been warned about Salihan in the past, and Alimu had been all but ignoring me since I told him I was pregnant, but I had a hard time wrapping my brain around Yonus acting this way. He had been so kind and caring before and seemed like an upstanding person. Now, he didn't seem any better than his brother.

There was still one thing I hadn't tried, one place I hadn't been, one place that I needed to go. Alimu's home. I had his address with me on the photo of his license, and I needed to have a heart-to-heart with his mother and stepfather anyway to see how much they wanted to be involved in the baby's life. Maybe they could help get the money situation sorted, too. If they would be able to make Alimu or Yonus or whoever give me the money, then I could fly home as soon as my cats were travel-ready, and if they couldn't help me, well, then I figured I would have to swallow my pride and ask my parents for help.

I didn't tell anybody outside of Xining what my plan was. I didn't want anyone to talk me out of it, and I was fairly certain that my friends were tired of this drama, anyway. I called JunGe and asked if he would be willing to drive me up to YangLong, a thirteen-hour-long journey one way. I told him I would pay for gas, food, and accommodation, since we would have to stop somewhere overnight. He agreed to take me but had a few errands to take care of the next day, so we made a plan to leave late the next afternoon. If it weren't for JunGe, I would have needed to hire a driver, which would have cost me handsomely. JunGe really was doing this out of the kindness of his heart. I would like to think that me being a foreigner had nothing to do with it, but I think the reality is that my foreign status made my Hui friends hurt for me and pushed them to go out of their way for me. Perhaps I am wrong, though, and the big hearts of my friends would open for anyone in need. I want to believe the latter.

I decided not to tell any of Alimu's family that I was coming either. I was afraid they'd tell Alimu, and I didn't want him to be there when I showed up. I wanted time alone with his parents to tell my side of the story, and I was interested in hearing what they had to say without Alimu present. Of course, it was always possible that he'd already headed back to YangLong, but that was a possibility I would just have to live with.

Chapter 21

The scenery I saw on the way to YangLong literally brought me to tears. I remember one mountain peak in particular, rocky grey and capped with snow, that jutted up between the smaller, sedge-covered mountains on either side. In front of the mountain lay the plains of the steppe, full of yak and sheep, and in front of the plain roared a mountain stream, glistening clear and sparkling like diamonds as the water tumbled carelessly over the boulders in its path. By this time of year, the flowers had all faded and the grasses were on their last legs of retaining their greenness before hibernating over the winter months. As we neared the end of the first day on the road, the sunset shone hues of bright pinks and oranges that kissed the tops of the mountains goodnight.

We stopped to rest that night right outside the town of Menyuan, about three hours away from Xining. We hadn't gotten far, but if we drove all day the next day, we could reach YangLong by 4:00pm. That was our plan, anyway. JunGe pulled over in front of a LanZhou pulled noodle restaurant for guaranteed halal food. Inside, the noodle-puller was ecstatic to meet a foreigner. He poured my tea, which was deep amber in color and incredibly salty. This was a specialty of the region that took some getting used to. I asked for a plate of boiled goat dumplings, and the noodle-puller, whose name was XiaoTong, bounded off to the kitchen to make them.

When our food was ready, XiaoTong asked to sit with us. JunGe looked annoyed, but I said I didn't mind. XiaoTong asked what I was doing all the way out in Qinghai, and I told him I was looking for someone who owed me money. XiaoTong laughed. "Then I wish you lots of success," he grinned, and left us to our meal. Later, XiaoTong asked me to add his contact information on WeChat. I agreed, thinking it would be nice to have someone new to talk to on the way up to YangLong. Little did I know, this was the start of a life-long friendship with XiaoTong.

We left the next morning at seven a.m. XiaoTong sent us off with a breakfast of steamed *mantou* buns and hard-boiled eggs. The journey was mostly silent. JunGe and I had already talked about everything we could think of, and now I was tired again. I kept falling asleep for long stretches, waking up every so often to take in the new landscape that appeared outside my window before drifting off again, eyes gazing up at clouds that sometimes formed so low, they enveloped the mountain tops.

It was late afternoon when we rolled into YangLong, but the GPS system was having a hard time navigating us to Alimu's home address. At one point, we turned around and headed outside of town, aiming for a dirt road that led to a series of small farmhouses pushed up against a dusty mountain. These people were not Alimu. We tried another road that GPS was confident of, but again we were led astray. Eventually, I had the idea of going back to town and simply asking around. Besides his address, I had plenty of pictures of Alimu, so surely somebody would recognize him and point us in the right direction.

This plan worked so well, I felt a little silly for not thinking of it sooner. JunGe drove us back into the town and aimed for the concrete courtyard in the middle of a block of houses. We pulled up alongside a man in a white shirt and black pants walking down the street, and I waved him over.

"Do you know where Alimu lives?" I asked, holding up my phone with a zoomed-in photo of Alimu's face.

"Ah, Ma Nai!" exclaimed the man, "Yeah, he lives over here!" And he began walking towards a house in the back row.

"I'll be right back," I said as I turned to JunGe, then left him in the car as I ran after the man in white.

Once I clearly saw which house the man was pointing to, I went back to JunGe to retrieve my backpack and tell him where to park.

"I'm going to head back now," he said.

"You're leaving?" I asked, a bit shocked. I realized then that I hadn't technically asked for a round-trip ride, and although I had assumed that JunGe would wait for me until I was done with Alimu's family, my assumption was wrong!

"It's a long way back," JunGe said, "and I want to be back in Xining tomorrow. You should be able to catch a bus from here, don't worry."

With that, he left. I stood hesitantly, watching him leave, feeling like there was absolutely no turning back now. Whether I wanted to or not, the only place to go from here was to Alimu's house. I turned and walked towards the house the man had pointed to, although I didn't see him around anymore. All of the houses were small, and short brick walls were built up around the front yards of each house, forming a courtyard for each family. As I approached the entrance of Alimu's courtyard, I was greeted by a rather frantic looking Qiong and Kelimu.

"Anna! What are you doing here?" Qiong said with a look of surprise in her eyes.

"I'm here to talk to Alimu's parents about the baby," I said. "And I want my money back, too."

"You really can't talk to our parents now," Kelimu said. "My father is resting, and my mother is at work."

"Well then I can wait until your father wakes up," I protested.

"No, not without Alimu," Qiong said. "Their father doesn't speak very good *Putonghua* (the common Mandarin dialect) and you need someone to help explain what's going on."

"Well then you can explain what's going on," I stated, spreading my stance.

"If you go in there now, it's just going to lead to confusion and anger," Kelimu said, "and you don't want to have my father angry at you. But once Alimu is here, we can all go in together and sit down for a civil conversation. Trust me."

I sighed, but agreed to wait for Alimu before speaking with his parents. What choice did I have? Rushing headlong into the house would solve nothing, especially if the father couldn't speak the common tongue. I had no clue how long we would have to wait for Alimu, and it seemed like they didn't have any clue either. The first thing they did was hurry me away to Kelimu's truck. I sat in the front seat while Qiong sat in the small back seat, and we drove to the outskirts of town, stopping on a hill between the city limits and the open highway. Kelimu got out and made a phone call, pacing up and down the middle of the road as he spoke.

When the call ended, he climbed back inside the truck.

"Where are we going?" I asked.

"We're going to see Su'erdai," he said. "She and her husband live here now."

We then drove a small way down the road, less than a mile's jaunt, and turned down a dirt path that led to a long farmhouse. Kelimu instructed me to wait in the truck while he and Qiong went inside. They returned about ten minutes later but said nothing to me as we turned around and drove away. We drove another mile before turning right onto another dirt road that soon turned to gravel. This road was headed up to the mountains, and the small truck had a rough go over the rocky terrain. The air grew even thinner as we climbed higher, and I found it harder to breathe with the jostling of the truck. Up ahead, I could see a creek flowing down the mountain, and the truck turned left to follow the creek's bend. As soon as we turned, I could see a small but roaring waterfall straight ahead of us, and on the outcrop above that was a large, green canvas tent.

The tent was rectangular in shape with a black stove pipe barely sticking up through the center of the structure. Similar to a yurt, these types of herding tents were designed to be easily erected and disassembled for the nomadic lifestyle that was required of a great deal of yak herders. As we pulled up to the tent, Su'erdai emerged from inside. She opened my door and beckoned me to come with her. I complied, and Qiong, Kelimu, Su'erdai, and myself all piled into the tent.

There was room enough for all of us to sit comfortably, although we sat on small stools that were barely a foot and a half off the ground. These small stools were common in China, and I was used to sitting on them, knees practically touching my chest, from the endless nights of street barbeque in Jinan. A small table was set up to act as a counter for cooking supplies. A large, scorched tea kettle sat on top of a wood-burning stove in the middle of the room, and at the far end of the tent was a mattress and quilt big enough for two. The inside of the tent was warm enough that we could all take off our jackets, although nobody took advantage of the heat, and we remained bundled up to escape the crisp autumn air that still wafted in from under the woolen blankets hung up as flaps for the door.

"I'm going to go call Alimu," Kelimu said, and he made his way outside.

"Can't he just call from inside the tent?" I asked.

"No," Su'erdai replied. "There's no service up here. He has to go back down to the road if he wants to make a call."

I checked my phone, and there was indeed no service. My battery was running low, too, so I decided to turn it off. It would be useless if it was completely dead, and it was practically useless now without service. I slipped my phone into my jacket pocket and zipped it shut.

"My husband will be here soon," Su'erdai said. "His name is MaJun."

I chuckled, "I know so many Hui men with the name 'Jun'," I said.

Su'erdai chuckled, too. "His *jun* means 'army', so at least it's not the same character."

She made small talk with me, but she didn't ask me why I was in YangLong and said nothing about her brother. She poured the three of us a cup of tea, and we waited for Kelimu to return.

When Kelimu made his way back inside the tent, he sat down next to Qiong and they began talking in agitated tones. They spoke in *Qinghai Hua*, so any hope of my knowing what they were saying was lost. I could pick up a few familiar words here and there and I could tell they were talking about Alimu, but I didn't know the context, or even if it was good or bad. I sat silently, clutching my tea, glancing between the three of them until they stopped and turned to me.

"Alimu is on his way here," Kelimu said. "Once he gets here, we'll go down and talk to my parents, okay?"

"Okay," I agreed and continued to sit quietly on my stool.

Chapter 22

I don't remember eating that night or at any point in time during my stay in the tent, although I don't believe that Alimu's family let me go without meals. Whether or not I was fed, I don't know, but I know that the wait for Alimu had me hungrier than what was offered. I sipped on a liter of water throughout the hours on Su'erdai's insistence. She was worried that the thin air would get to my head and make me feel unwell. When I had to pee, she showed me the best place to straddle the edge of the small cliff near where the tent sat. MaJun had joined us before the evening turned to night, and now the tent held all five of us, all eagerly awaiting Alimu.

Occasionally, Kelimu would get a text message. His phone had enough reception to receive them, wavering between a single bar of service and no service at all. Sometimes it was from Alimu. Twice it was from Yonus. Everyone wanted to know the story of how and when I got pregnant, and they all seemed shocked to learn that we had sex in the car outside the hotel. They then asked to know everything that happened after I told Alimu I was pregnant and why I'd chosen to come to YangLong. I laid it all out on the table for them very frankly and tried to editorialize as little as possible. They said nothing to me in response, however, and just nodded their heads in acknowledgement. I asked more questions about Alimu, what he'd been doing and where my money was, but they could only say that they weren't involved in his situations and knew nothing of the matter.

I was tired of sitting in the tent and grew more anxious with each passing hour. How long would it be until Alimu got here? Nobody seemed to be able to give me a rough estimate. Would we still be talking to his parents this late at night? It was well past dinner time now. The thin air made me sleepy, and my legs ached from sitting on the little stool for so long.

It was after midnight by the time Alimu arrived. When we went outside to meet him, I saw that the front driver's side of his little red car was all dented in. Alimu was speaking angrily with Qiong and Kelimu, then he walked over to me.

"Do you see what happened to my car?!" he exclaimed harshly.

"How did that happen?" I asked.

"I was speeding up here because of YOU, and I hit a yak!" he said, obviously agitated.

I was annoyed at the "because of you" statement and fired back. "Well maybe you should have been a better driver!"

"What is wrong with you?" Alimu shouted. "My car gets destroyed and instead of asking if I'm okay, you just tell me to be a better driver? Don't you care at all?"

I immediately felt guilty. I hadn't even been concerned about him. He looked fine, but wouldn't someone who truly loved him think to ask if he were okay? And I didn't even do that, I was too caught up in myself! "I'm sorry," I said. "Are you okay?"

"I'm fine," he said, and seemed to calm down. "But the car will be expensive to fix. Come on, let's go inside the tent. It's freezing out here."

So, we all followed Alimu into the tent. Frost had already formed on the grass, crunching softly beneath our shoes as we walked back inside. Su'erdai pulled out another stool and we situated ourselves.

"How do you know where I live? Why are you here bothering my family?" Alimu began to question.

"I have your address from your driver's license. You sent me the photo. I'm here because I need my money and I need to know if your parents want anything to do with the baby," I said.

"They don't!" he shouted. "Believe me, I know! They're just going to tell you to get an abortion and then get mad at me. They don't want anything to do with you."

"I'm NOT having an abortion," I growled. Alimu jumped to his feet and grabbed the metal teapot from the stove, lunging towards me. Before he could reach me, Su'erdai stood and grabbed the teapot from him then pointed outside and spoke harshly to him. I assume she was ordering him out to cool off, because he then left the tent. She placed the teapot down and asked if I was all right. Upon my confirmation, she and the others followed him outside.

I could hear them arguing through the tent walls and decided not to get in the middle of it. But I couldn't stand being by myself for very long and soon worked up the courage to go intrude. As I stepped outside, I instinctually looked up at the stars, an old habit I picked up from living rurally back home, and what I saw made me gasp. Millions of bright stars were bursting through the night sky, shining with a brilliance I'd never seen before. The Milky Way flowed like a river of white across a canopy of deep blue-black, and with no moon, I saw more constellations, clusters, and foreign bodies than I'd ever seen before or since. I have always longed to be among the stars, and seeing them with such clarity felt akin to an out-of-body experience.

I didn't have long to take in the experience, however, as Alimu grabbed my arm and pulled me towards his car declaring that he wanted to talk to me alone. He opened the back seat door and motioned for me to get in.

"We're not going anywhere," he said. "It's too cold to stay outside and talk."

I got inside the car, and Alimu walked around to the other side, climbed in and slid closer to me until our bodies touched.

"What do you want to say?" I asked him.

"Me? What do YOU want to say? You're the one who came all the way here," he spoke, lowering his voice to a gentle and almost playful tone.

"I really need my money, Alimu, and I need to talk to your family," I said.

"Okay, okay, you can talk to my family tomorrow," he said. "It's too late to go there now. They're all asleep. When we wake up tomorrow, we'll take you down there and we can talk as a group."

"Thank you," I told him, noticing that he'd said nothing further about the money, but I was too tired to try to fight about it then. There would be plenty of time to hash it all out tomorrow, I thought to myself.

Alimu leaned his body closer to mine. "Are you cold?" he asked.

"No, I'm fine," I told him, though in truth I was trying my hardest not to shiver.

We sat in silence momentarily before Alimu exited the car. He came back around to my car door and opened it for me.

"Come on, let's go get some sleep," he said, and he motioned towards the tent.

I didn't have anything else to say to Alimu that night. I'd only been repeating myself the past few weeks, like a broken record, and I was ready for this all to be over. Tomorrow would be the last step I'd need to take before going home. Su'erdai and Qiong had already pulled out pillows and blankets, and it was decided that the women would sleep inside the tent while the men slept in their vehicles. The bed wasn't big enough for all of us, and giving up the warm and comfortable spot was the polite thing to do. We all slipped into bed that night wearing our clothes from the day. I took my phone out of my jacket pocket and slipped it in between the tent wall and the mattress on the ground. I didn't want anyone to take it and rifle around in it, and I wasn't sure if Alimu might try something funny like that. To my surprise, I felt something cold and wet touch my hand. I looked over to find a beer bottle tucked in the same hiding spot as my phone. I smiled, knowing that this was either MaJun or Su'erdai's little secret, most likely the former, and it wasn't my place to out them.

When I woke up the next morning, I found the beer bottle again. Frost had formed on the outside of the bottle, despite the blazing fire in the wood-burning stove. I turned on my phone to check for service, but was disappointed to see there was still nothing. Looking around, I was surprised to find the tent completely empty. I straightened my clothes and walked to the door of the tent. I listened. And I heard nothing. I was unsure if I should stay inside or go outside and try to find the group, but I was tired of sitting on a little stool. I wanted to stretch my legs and get a good look around.

Su'erdai had warned me the day before not to stay out in the sun too long. At this high of an altitude, I would be easily sunburned. As I stood on the cliff outside the tent, staring off into the mountains in the distance, I felt the sun beat down on my face, warming my skin. It was still cold enough to need a jacket, but the sun's rays were in fact intense, and I wondered if I shouldn't take Su'erdai's warning more seriously.

Turning around, I could see the four siblings up on top of a hill behind me. Alimu had fashioned himself a lasso, throwing it around the necks of the goats that Qiong and Su'erdai herded his way. I saw him land one, and Kelimu rushed over to load the caught goat into the bed of his truck. It was a holiday that day for the Hui people, celebrated first by sacrificing and later eating the goats. When three goats had been tied and loaded in the truck, Kelimu and Qiong left down the mountain. Su'erdai came up to me, noting how the sun had already begun to burn my face, urging me back inside the tent. I complied to make her feel happy. As she began to follow me back inside the tent, Alimu grabbed her arm, speaking to her in a low voice. He pulled her to the side of the tent, and she let the cotton flaps close.

After some time had passed, Su'erdai came back inside. "Alimu wants to speak with you," she told me, and began tending to the tea. I left the tent.

Alimu waved me over to sit with him on a plastic water tank.

"Look, Anna…" he began, "I really want to talk to you."

"Okay, I'm listening," I said, crossing my arms.

"I'm just so sorry," he said, "for everything. I love you, I really do, but I've just been terrified ever since you told me you were pregnant. There's nothing more I'd like in the world than t o start a family with you, but now is just not the right time."

He stared at me for a moment, as if he were letting me digest what he was saying. Then he continued, "My mom and stepfather are very traditional. Sex outside of marriage is considered a grave sin, and they would never condone a baby out of wedlock. If we went to them right now and told them you were pregnant, they would kick both of us out and never speak to us again!"

"That doesn't mean you have to be such a jerk about it," I said, tears forming in my eyes.

"Anna, I *want* to be with you," he said. "I want to be with you no matter what, but we can't do that if we have this baby. Do you know why I was so late getting here yesterday? I was looking for an apartment for us in Xining, and I found one. It's furnished and not too expensive, and all I need to do is call the landlord. I want you to move in with me. We'll go to Jinan together and collect your belongings. You can say goodbye to your friends, and then we can start our life, right here in Qinghai."

I stared at him in disbelief. But I didn't know what to say. He went on, "We all have to make sacrifices in life, eventually everybody has to sacrifice something. I'm asking you, please Anna, make this one sacrifice. Agree to an abortion. I'll be with you the whole time, and it will make way for us to be together, for us to meet my parents properly, get married, and have as many children as we want! We can have ten kids if you want! But I'm asking you, please, Anna, make this sacrifice for us, for our family. I'm so sorry for the way I've treated you. I let my fear stop me from being the man I need to be, but from today on out, I promise to be there for you no matter what."

I couldn't believe what I was hearing. I sat there processing everything Alimu just told me, trying to take it all in and make sense of it. He was offering me everything I wanted, not just an apology but a whole life with him. It wasn't just me that wanted him, but he wanted me, too. I could understand him being terrified, because I was terrified, too. Then he reached for my hand.

"I know you want this baby. I want this baby, too," he said. "It will come back to us when we're ready." Then he smiled at me and tucked a loose dreadlock behind my ear.

I told him I would have to think about it before making my decision. He told me he understood. I wanted to talk to Su'erdai. Alimu fetched her from the tent and left us alone together.

She joined me on the plastic container. I told her everything that Alimu had just told me, and I asked her what she thought of his proposal. "Wait a second," she told me, "I have to talk to him." And she went back into the tent to find Alimu.

She emerged a few minutes later. "Well, do you believe him?" I asked her.

"I… do…" she said slowly, nodding her head, "I think he's telling you the truth."

"Then I have some serious thinking to do," I told her, and decided to get back out of the sun.

Alimu stood up as I reentered the tent. "Well?" he asked.

"Let me think," I told him. "This isn't easy."

"I have some work to do," he told me. "So you stay here. Don't go out in the sun, you'll burn, okay? We were born here, so we're used to it, but you need to be careful."

I nodded and he left. Su'erdai followed not long after, needing to tend to her herds of yaks and goats on the hillside. I was alone in the tent once more. I slipped my hand into my pocket and wrapped my fingers tightly around my phone. If only I had service, I thought to myself, maybe I could talk to Samm about this, but Samm was too far away to help me this time and the decision between life as a single mother and life with Alimu was one that I would have to face all on my own.

Chapter 23

I spent two hours sitting by myself in the tent, running around in circles in my head. What was the right choice? Could I even live with myself if I had an abortion? I hadn't started feeling movement yet, but it was going to start happening any day now... I was well into my second trimester. My dream was to be with Alimu, but at what cost? I decided to go for a walk to clear my head. I walked down off the cliff and found the waterfall I'd seen before. I stuck my hands in the water just downstream from the froth and was surprised at how cold it was, immediately chilling my hands like ice. Digging around in the rocks with my shoe, I searched for anything that would catch my eye. Maybe there would be a special treasure from the earth.

Soon, I saw Alimu walk up beside me.

"I thought I told you to stay in the tent," he said. "You're going to burn out here, you're too high up."

"I just needed to think," I said, then added hesitantly, "I need to talk to your parents before I make my decision."

"That's a bad idea," Alimu said. "I can handle them if I'm just telling them about our relationship, but if we walk in and say we're pregnant, they aren't going to want to listen to anything you have to say. They're just going to kick you out immediately. My stepfather is not a kind man."

He then went on, "We can't leave the mountain until Kelimu and Qiong get back with the truck, and they won't be back until the evening. You have plenty of time to keep thinking. I have to get back to work now." With that, he walked back up the mountain.

I don't recall eating any meals that day, although I'm certain I was somehow fed. I remember Alimu and Su'erdai picking up two dozen eggs from a bag and shaking them individually to see if they were still good. I do not remember if Su'erdai cooked with those eggs. All I can remember is sitting and thinking about my options. I wasn't a fan of any of the choices that lay ahead of me. Was I being irresponsible by wanting to keep this baby? Was I being selfish? Alimu was serious enough about us that he'd already found an apartment and was ready to move in. Moreover, things were different in China; it wasn't like the US, where single-parent homes were normal. There was a lot of shame and stigma around having a baby out of wedlock, and his parents were willing to turn their backs on all of us if it was born.

I had previously been so against having an abortion. I truly didn't want one, but that was before Alimu told me that he really did love me, and that he had just been frightened and he had carved out a path for us to be together. I felt sick to my stomach. Neither decision felt right, and everything around me felt so wrong. How did it all come to this, stuck on a mountain facing the hardest decision of my life? I needed to find Alimu again.

"I can't do this by myself..." I told him, my voice trailing off as I stared him in the eyes.

"I know," he said, his brow softening. "I'm going to be with you. I'm not going to leave you ever again."

"Do you promise?" I asked.

"Of course. I promise!" he said.

Hearing this final commitment, I decided that the most logical choice was to go through with the abortion. I couldn't rely on my heart to make the decision for me. I would have to make a big sacrifice, the biggest sacrifice of my life, but it would all be for my future family with Alimu. We could bring honor to the child we didn't have through our love for the children we would have in the future, and Alimu promised he would stick with me through it all. With his support, I could do it. It wouldn't be easy, but knowing he would be by my side gave me strength.

When I told him my decision, he replied with a softly spoken, "okay." I asked Su'erdai what decision she would make. She responded she would make the same decision I did. That made me feel better. She was the only other woman I could talk to, and she seemed to truly care about me. She knew her culture, her parents, and her brother much more intimately than I did, ultimately, so I took her guidance to heart.

I had spent practically all day in the tent by myself, and it was late evening by the time Kelimu and Qiong returned. The four of them engaged in a bustling conversation I couldn't understand before Kelimu and Qiong headed back to their truck, and Su'erdai began to grab my bag. Alimu told me it was time to leave and escorted me to his car, opening the back seat for me to sit in, but before getting in, I was struck by the sudden urge to pee, so I excused myself for the nearby cliff.

Before I could make my way back to the car, MaJun cut me off in my path.

"Anna, I don't trust Alimu," MaJun said. "I can't tell what exactly he's lying about, but he's lying about something. So, be careful, okay? Here." He pushed a twenty-yuan bill into my hand. "For snacks," he said, and forced a smile. I wasn't sure what to say to him other than to thank him for his words and for the money. Then I climbed into Alimu's car and put a hand up to give MaJun a single wave. The car headed down the mountain in front of the truck, just in case it ended up getting stuck. But Alimu cleared the mountain road with little trouble, and we soon found ourselves back in town.

"Are we going to talk to your parents now?" I asked Alimu.

"No," he replied. "We don't want my stepfather finding out you're pregnant, but my mom wants to talk to you so we're going to go pick her up."

We waited on the opposite side of the town's courtyard next to Alimu's house. Alimu turned the car off, and the headlights faded. Soon, the front passenger door opened, and his mother slid inside. They chatted in low, soft voices, with Alimu gesturing back to me with his head. His mother turned around to face me. *Xiexie* (thank you) she said in a heavily accented voice, and stuck a fifty yuan bill out for me to take. I initially tried to refuse, although I knew that doing so for too long would be considered rude, so I took the money after the second insistence. Then she left the car and Alimu turned to me.

"If my stepfather catches her outside the house or if he knew that she paid you that much money, he would be very mad at her, but she insisted on seeing you," Alimu told me.

Then we left town. We drove until almost midnight. I assumed that we were heading back towards Xining, but the town we stopped in didn't seem familiar. I was too tired to pay much mind, though. Kelimu and Qiong pulled in behind us, and we poured into the hotel, securing two rooms. Again, the men and women slept separately. I was finally able to charge my phone and take a shower, but sleep didn't come easily that night and I tossed and turned until the sun broke through the eastern window. I again have no memory of the meal we ate that night, if we ate at all, or of our breakfast the next morning. In fact, I barely remember the car ride to the hospital, except that it just didn't look familiar at all. Still, I didn't ask where we were going. I didn't want to think too much about it, I just wanted it to be over.

We pulled into a small city around noon, heading straight to the hospital. The roads and buildings were coated with orange and red dust from the sands that resulted from desertification in the area. People were scarce here, with only a few cars in the street and even fewer carts and bikes on the road. I followed behind the group as we walked into the hospital, trying to catch a sign of what city we were in, but I had no such luck. After speaking with the nursing staff downstairs, we were led upstairs to meet with the doctor. There was nobody in the waiting room, and the doctor motioned us into her private office. Alimu and Su'erdai spoke with her first. I couldn't understand what they were saying.

As they continued to have their conversation, I was growing more and more anxious. "I can tell you what I want!" I spoke out, eyes clenched. I tried my best to explain to the doctor that I wanted to take the abortion pill then be put under anesthesia for a D&E, but nobody could quite figure out what I was saying, and my vocabulary wasn't sufficient to include these medical terms. I tried to speak as simply as possible.

"I want to take the pill, then the doctor makes me go to sleep, then the doctor goes inside and takes the baby out," I tried to explain.

"You want a C-section?!" Qiong exclaimed.

"No! Not that…" I began to cry as I tried to correctly spell the word "anesthesia" on the Chinese-English dictionary app on my phone, but I was so frazzled that I kept misspelling it.

Eventually, the doctor caught on to what I was saying and ran through the scenario with me. When I confirmed that's what I wanted, they told Alimu that it would cost extra to have me sedated. Otherwise, they would have me deliver the baby via a normal vaginal birth, which would be much cheaper. I told Alimu that I already had to give up my baby's life, I didn't want to have to birth it, too. I should note here that parents in China are not allowed to know the gender of their babies before birth, and I was no exception. Therefore, I did not know if my child was a boy or a girl, but I knew giving birth to that baby would be too much for my heart to bear, so Alimu paid for the procedure to be carried out in the manner I'd specified.

The doctor then took me into a private room and handed me a pill and a glass of water. "You'll take the first one now," she said, "then take the second one tomorrow when you come back here. You'll need to be here by noon."

I stood with the pill in one hand and the water in the other, looking out the window, wondering if I was truly making the right choice.

"This is it," I thought to myself. "There's no going back now. Once you make this decision, there won't be any do-overs." Then Alimu walked over and placed his hand on my back. I placed the pill on my tongue and drank the water.

Chapter 24

I tried to hold back my tears as we left the hospital. Everybody was acting like this was no big deal. In a way, to them, it wasn't a big deal. Abortions were commonplace in China, and I knew many women who'd had one and talked about it openly, as if it were just another medical procedure. Perhaps that's how it should be everywhere, but they were probably fine with terminating their pregnancies. I was not. I had always been pro-choice, but I still wasn't convinced that the choice I made was the right one.

In any case, it was too late to go back now, and my tummy gurgled with hunger. Alimu and Su'erdai split off from the group. Qiong and Kelimu stayed with me.

"Where are they going?" I asked.

"They have to figure out how much it will cost to fix Alimu's car," Kelimu said, "and we need to find a hotel room for the night."

"And we're taking you to dinner," Qiong said. "What would you like to eat?"

"Goat dumplings," I responded, knowing that a pulled noodle restaurant would be safe for them to eat at while also serving delicious dumplings.

But when we got to the restaurant, I could barely eat. The dumplings smelled divine and tasted even better, but trying to make them slide down my throat felt like suffocating. Qiong and Kelimu urged me to eat more, but I couldn't even finish half my plate. Kelimu ate the rest. After dinner, it was a short walk to our hotel. Su'erdai was already there, but Alimu was still away. Unfortunately, I had no time to rest. Since the hotel had a stable Wi-Fi connection, I desperately needed to get some homework done. For the past few months, I'd been working on my bachelor's degree online. I was already several days late submitting projects in two of my classes, and midterms were right around the corner. I desperately wanted to just lie on the bed and wait for Alimu to return, but I knew I needed to get to work.

My laptop's charging cable had to be plugged in to an outlet near a far corner of the room, and I situated myself on the floor. Unfortunately, I found that this week's project involved creating a visual diagram to submit. I didn't have the time or the patience to create anything digitally, and all I had with me in the hotel room was a small pad of paper and a pen. So, I created a diagram of my chosen biome with extremely crude drawings on a 6x8 inch piece of paper. Although the assignment felt more suited for a high school classroom, I knew the high school version of myself would have been disappointed with my results.

I stopped for a break and looked out the window, trying to find a sign that might identify what town we were in. Finally, I spotted a billboard featuring an ad for the town's local nature attraction. We were in JiuQuan, a small city of less than a million people in northwestern Gansu province. We had traveled in the opposite direction from Xining, but why?

I asked Su'erdai, "Why didn't we go to Xining for this?"

"JiuQuan is closer," she said. "It's only six hours from home, but driving to Xining is almost twelve hours. Plus, we're a lot lower in elevation here, so it'll be easier for you to breathe."

Then Su'erdai and Qiong both exited the women's hotel room to talk privately in the men's room across the hall. Kelimu came in, asking to talk to me.

"You're not alone in this," he told me. "Qiong and I had to go through this, too. But she was eight months pregnant. We tried to run away together and have the baby, but our families told us they would disown us if we didn't come back and get an abortion. I held that little baby in my arms…" and he began to cry. My heart broke for him. I was struggling enough at four months, I couldn't fathom trying to go through this at eight months, when your baby is practically here. I didn't know what to say to him aside from "I'm sorry that happened," and that just didn't feel like enough.

Teary-eyed, Kelimu stood up and walked out of the room. As soon as he left, Qiong came back inside and sat on the bed closest to me. She told me that tonight, she and Kelimu wanted to share a bed, instead of separating ourselves by genders.

"Qiong, I know what's going to happen," I said.

"What's going to happen?" she questioned, curiously.

"Alimu is going to tell me that I need to get lots of rest tonight and, for my health, it's best if I sleep alone. And he's going to leave me alone again tonight, I just know it!" I told her.

I didn't care if Qiong and Kelimu shared a bed, but if we were going to separate into couples, I didn't want to be alone, and I had a gut feeling I was going to be left out of this one.

"I don't think that will happen," Qiong said reassuringly. Later, when Alimu finally came back, I saw Qiong intercept him in the hallway. Although they spoke in *Qinghai Hua*, I could pick out Qiong saying my name and the word for "sleep", and I was almost certain that Qiong was telling Alimu what I'd told her. It made me feel angry. I didn't want Alimu to feel compelled to sleep in the bed with me. I wanted him to do it because he wanted to. I just wasn't a fan of the mentality that those going through a difficult time needed to rest alone.

That night, Alimu lay in bed with me and scrolled through the pictures on my phone.

"Anna, I want you to delete all the pictures you have of me, okay?" he said to me.

"Why?" I asked.

"I don't really want my pictures out in the world anymore. I'm going to take them off QQ and ask my family to delete their pictures, too," he responded.

I knew that if I deleted my pictures from my photo gallery, I could recover them from my trash files later. I didn't want to delete them, but I wanted to make Alimu happy. I decided to delete them for now, then recover them later and transfer them to my computer for personal safe keeping. I knew that wasn't the respectful thing to do, and that if I had asked for my pictures to be deleted, I would expect total compliance, but at the time it felt like losing something that I wasn't quite ready to let go of.

Sleep was hard to find that night, but I dared not toss and turn, lest I wake up Alimu, who was snoring next to me. The next day came early, and I woke up to find everybody fussing about, trying to get ready for the day. Suddenly, Qiong, Kelimu, and Su'erdai began to tell me goodbye.

"Goodbye?!" I cried. "I thought you were going to stay! Qiong? Su'erdai?"

"We're sorry, Anna," Qiong said, "but we all need to get back home. There's lots of work that needs to be done, but Alimu is with you. He'll take good care of you. We'll see you soon in Xining." With that, the three of them left.

"I'm going to take you to the hospital a little early," Alimu said, forgoing breakfast for the both of us.

Arriving back at the hospital, I couldn't help but notice how empty the facility was. Despite its vast main lobby and open hallways, we were one of only a handful of patients. This was highly unusual compared to my experiences with hospitals in Jinan. We met the doctor from before, and she led us to a room at the end of a long hallway. The room had two beds inside, and a large curtainless window let in a flood of light. Alimu had paid extra for me to have a private room, and I appreciated the kindness. The last thing I wanted was a stranger in the room with me.

The doctor instructed me to change into a gown and lie on the bed nearest the window. Then a nurse brought me a pillow and a blanket. This was a rarity in Chinese hospitals, as most patients must bring their own pillows, blankets, clothes, food, and water. Alimu pulled a chair up beside the bed and sat next to me. Soon, the doctor came back with a pill and a bottle of water.

"This will dilate your cervix and make the baby come out," she explained. "It should take a couple of hours to start to work. Once that happens, we'll get you into surgery." Then she handed me the pill. I swallowed it as fast as I could, wanting to get the whole thing over with. And then… it hadn't even been fifteen minutes before I started to feel something happening. It started in my fingertips. Every single tip began hurting, first just a dull throb, but it soon turned into a burning pain that had me calling for the doctors. The fiery pain lasted a good twenty minutes, but by the time a doctor came in to see me, the pain had subsided. I still don't know why they were so slow to respond.

Another twenty minutes passed, and I began to feel cramping in my uterus. Like my fingertips, the pain started as a dull ache but soon began to grow in magnitude until I was gasping from the pain. I questioned why this was happening so soon. Wasn't it supposed to take hours? It was the most intense pain that I'd ever felt, and I began groaning, rolling from side to side trying to quell the fire on the inside. Eventually the pain got so bad that I began crying out.

"Something's not right," I told Alimu. "I need help."

"It hasn't been two hours yet, you still have time," he told me, but I insisted that he find a nurse.

They transferred me into another room closer to the nurse's station, but the pain was unbearable and I was bellowing in pain, tears streaming down my face. I was waiting for someone, anyone, to come in and check on me, but nobody came. I felt like I was waiting forever, pushing through the pain as best as I could, hot tears blurring my eyes. Then Alimu came into the room and squatted down next to the bed.

"Anna," he said to me softly, "if you don't calm down, the doctors won't come in. They don't believe you're in this much pain, and I don't believe it either. Stop screaming, stop crying, and then someone will help you."

I was so taken aback. Doctors in China aren't always patient-focused like they are in the US, and things like good bedside manner and making sure your patient is comfortable weren't high priorities in this hospital. I bit down hard on the inside of my cheeks and held my breath, trying to breathe through the pain. The nurses had me move back to my private room and lay back down on the bed. A few minutes later, a nurse came in to check my cervix. Immediately, her eyes widened.

"We have to get you into surgery, now!" she cried, and she rushed out of the room to find the doctor.

The doctor escorted me from my private room to the surgical room, which consisted of a large gynecological chair with stirrups, an array of surgical instruments, and several electronic devices that I didn't recognize. Four doctors and nurses busied themselves helping me climb into the chair while arranging their tools. I was gritting my teeth in pain, trying not to scream. A nurse inserted an IV line into my arm, and I tried not to pass out. Blood, needles, and IVs all make me collapse if I'm not careful, and I didn't want to fall out of the chair. Alimu stayed beside me the whole time, taking my hand and rubbing my arm to comfort me. Soon, the anesthesiologist came to me.

"Do I get to sleep now?" I asked in a pleading voice.

He chuckled, "You sure do! We'll see you when you wake up." And with that, a nurse held a plastic mask over my face while the gas flooded into my nostrils. I felt the coolness of the anesthesia bleed into my veins, and then a slow darkness took over me and I was out.

Chapter 25

I tried to wake up, but I couldn't. I heard strange voices calling out my name. I felt hands on my cheeks, and I drifted from a semi-conscious state back into darkness. More voices came next, slightly frantic. One leaned down close to me. I could feel the voice's breath on my skin. "You need to wake up!"

I opened my eyes. I was still in the gynecological chair, completely reclined. The intense pain I felt before was replaced with a dull ache. Seeing I was now awake, the doctor and two nurses left. The remaining nurse turned to me.

"We're all done with the procedure. Nothing went wrong. I have to push on your belly now," she said, and she pushed down hard on my womb. I felt blood surging out of me, and I cried out in pain. I wasn't expecting that to hurt, and nobody told me why she had to do it, but she informed me that it would happen several more times and asked me to try to keep my pain to myself. Despite just completing the operation, the nurses had me walk down the long hallway back to my room. My legs felt like they could barely move, and I winced in pain with each step. Alimu walked beside me in silence.

As we turned into the room and I grabbed the bed, Alimu said to me, "I can't tell any difference between you being pregnant and you not being pregnant." I was so hurt! It was true that I was overweight, and I hadn't really started showing yet, but why did he have to make that comment? I was feeling so vulnerable already, and he said what I thought was the worst thing you could say to someone at a moment like this. As soon as I was situated in bed, Alimu told me he was leaving. He was going to get me something to eat. What I truly wanted was for him to stay next to me. Eating was the last thing on my mind. However, I knew that bringing food to someone in the hospital was a true sign of love and friendship, and culturally, it would be best to allow him to make this gesture. So Alimu left.

I laid on the bed and slept until he came back. I don't know how long he was away. When he returned, he carried a bag of cakes and bakery items. I was slightly disappointed. I was beginning to feel hungry now, and it was nice that he was thinking of me enough to buy me cake, but something hearty and savory sounded much better. Still, I didn't want to complain and thanked him for going out of his way. Alimu paced at the foot of my bed then turned to me.

"I have to go get the car fixed now," he said. "I'll be back in a few hours. Sorry to leave." And he walked out of the hospital without saying another word.

Sitting alone, I began to realize just exactly what I'd done. The fact that I had just killed my baby set in and emotions began to sweep over me. I felt so guilty and angry at myself. I should have just gone back home! It was too late now, and I'd have to lean on Alimu. I willed him back to my side, to be with me while I grieved, but he stayed gone. I decided to reach out to my family.

In my shame, I texted our group chat that I'd had a miscarriage and was now in the hospital recovering. My parents and siblings all felt deeply sorry for me, offering me condolences and comforting words, but there wasn't much to say, really, and I felt even guiltier for lying to them. I just couldn't stand to utter the truth about what I'd done. How long could I keep this secret inside of me? Could I bury this in my heart forever?

It took hours for Alimu to return. When he came inside my room, he immediately began pacing back and forth at the end of my bed. Then he stopped and moved to the side of my bed.

"I have something to tell you," he said firmly, looking at the wall.

"Okay…" I said, wondering if he had bad news about the car, but it was much worse than that.

"I'm married," he said. "I've been married since you told me you were pregnant. I went out and married someone so I couldn't be forced to marry you, and now, my wife just told me today she's pregnant, too."

I stared at Alimu, absolutely stunned. The very first thought that ran through my mind was, "Well I hope she has a miscarriage," immediately followed by, "No! The pain of losing a child shouldn't be wished on anyone!" I didn't want to believe he was actually married.

"Where is she? How have you been able to spend all this time with me?" I asked frantically.

"I left her in Qilian. I told her to stay there and wait for me. She does what I say." Alimu said sharply.

"What about our plan to move to Xining? I thought you loved me? You told me you loved me!" I cried out, tears bursting from my eyes.

"I did love you, once. I was going to divorce my wife and live with you. My plan was to stay with you instead of her, but now she's pregnant," Alimu said.

How could I believe him? He had lied to me about being married. Then I considered that he might not even be married but rather just lying about being married. He'd lied about everything else, so why not this, too! Was there ever really an apartment in Xining, or was Alimu just willing to say anything he could to make me hate him? Was he really married, or did he know he could get away with anything if he just said he had a wife? What about his family? Did Qiong and Kelimu and Su'erdai know about this the whole entire time? Why didn't somebody, anybody, tell me that he was married?

Well, in truth, somebody had told me he was married. Salihan told me when I came to Xining the second time, but that was before I was pregnant. So, was he married then and only Salihan would tell me the truth, or was he married after I got pregnant, and nobody told me the truth? Or maybe he wasn't married at all, so there was no more truth to tell? I felt like I was going crazy!

"You made me kill my baby!" I screamed at him. "I did it for you! I did it for us!"

"I could never let someone as disgusting as you have my child," he said angrily.

I didn't know what to say to that, so I said nothing. I sat staring at him in silence, my face red and wet with tears.

"I'll be back tomorrow," Alimu said, then turned around and walked out.

I sobbed harder than ever. Everything had been taken from me, and I gave up my baby for nothing! For absolutely nothing. There would be no happy ending to this story. My dreams were shattered, and I began to tremble with grief and anger. A nurse came in and hushed me.

"There are new mothers in the other rooms trying to rest with their babies. They don't want to listen to you crying!" she told me, adding insult to injury.

I lay in bed, body aching, silently crying until darkness fell. I was hungry now, but all I had were the last remnants of a pastry from earlier. It was then that I realized I'd seen the bakery yesterday next to the hospital. Alimu didn't give me cake because it was a nice gesture to cheer me up, he gave me cake because it was the cheapest and closest thing he could find without going out of his way. I only had half a bottle of water left, too, and no way of getting more unless someone could get it for me, and I had nobody in the hospital that would take on that task.

After hours of reproaching myself, I decided I couldn't hold the truth in any longer. I needed to tell my mother what had happened. Hands shaking, I picked up my cell phone to text her. I told her that I lied, that I didn't have a miscarriage, I'd had an abortion! I told her that I did it for Alimu so we could start a life together, only to find out he was married and it was all a sham. She comforted me the best she knew how, and I apologized for lying. I asked if she would be willing to tell my siblings the truth for me, but she told me that was something I needed to do on my own. I spoke with my brother first, then my sister. My brother was heartbroken that there would be no baby. My sister was heartbroken that I'd been put in that situation.

But there was someone else who was heartbroken, too. My ex-fiancé's ex-best friend, Thomas, had been keeping up with my journey in China, too. He didn't know much about Alimu, but he knew I was pregnant, and he knew I was coming home. We had known each other since I was sixteen, so we were far from strangers. Desperately wanting to have a family, he volunteered to raise the baby with me. Thomas had his own apartment and had already begun preparing financially for a child. When I told him about the abortion, I could sense that he was beyond angry with me. He had very little to say, except that he was disappointed in my choice. Perhaps I had let him down the most.

I didn't want to be alone that night, but I was too ashamed to reach out to anybody else. How could I face Samm and Katherine and tell them what I'd done? What would they think of me? How could they forgive my foolishness and ignorance? I somehow managed to find sleep that night, but that sleep was fraught with nightmares, and I woke before the dawn. Alimu came back not long after the sun had risen. He had more cake for breakfast.

"The car still isn't ready yet," he said, "so you're going to wait in the hotel. Come with me."

I slowly gathered up my belongings from the room and followed after him, intentionally keeping a distance. As we reached the end of the hallway, I heard a nurse running after us, shouting, "WAIT!"

The nurses and doctors all wanted a photo with me. I was the first foreign patient they'd ever treated at their hospital, and they wanted to commemorate the occasion. We stood in the lobby of the women's ward, and I let them position me front and center. Ten doctors and nurses all leaned in and smiled as the camera flashed. The nurse directly beside me held her hands up in a peace sign and grinned from ear to ear. When they were done, the group took turns shaking my hand. Everyone was happy. It was perhaps the most surreal experience of my life.

I followed Alimu outside and we began walking toward the hotel. Luckily, it was only a couple of blocks away. My body ached, and walking was uncomfortable. I wanted a cigarette badly and was in desperate need of water, but Alimu forbade me from stopping inside a convenience store to pick anything up.

"I'll get you what you need," he said in a flat, cold voice. "You still need to rest." I didn't feel like protesting and instead just followed his instructions.

He led me to the hotel room first before immediately turning around to head to the store downstairs. I ducked into the bathroom to check my bleeding. Thankfully, Alimu returned with a pack of extra-large pads, along with a bowl of pickled vegetable flavor instant noodles and a bottle of pear juice. Ironically, this was my least favorite flavor of instant noodles and my least favorite flavor of juice. He also bought me a pack of cigarettes, and I lit up as soon as he exited the hotel room again.

At least I could stop feeling guilty about smoking. It was only affecting *me* now, not anyone else. I sat on the bed in silence and chain-smoked two more, thinking about everything and nothing all at once. I didn't know how long Alimu would be gone, and he'd told me not to leave the hotel so we could leave as soon as his car was finished. I decided to try to watch some tv, and finding no English shows, I settled on a talent show featuring Gansu's best and brightest youth. I tried to eat the noodles, but the sour kick of the pickled vegetables was too much for me, and I couldn't get past the third bite.

It was noon before Alimu came back and hurried me to grab my belongings and get in his car. The dents were gone now, and the car had recently been waxed. I walked to the front passenger seat when Alimu stopped me.

"You need to sit in the back," he said. "I don't want to look at you."

I said nothing but climbed in the back seat.

Chapter 26

It was a nine-hour journey from JiuQuan to Xining. Alimu and I spent most of the ride in silence, him in the front and me in the back. At one point he looked back and asked me, "Why do you look so mad?"

"Because you made me kill my baby," I responded coldly.

"I didn't make you do anything," he said. "You wanted that abortion, you didn't want a baby. That was all your decision to make, not mine."

Tears welled up in my eyes as I bit down hard on my tongue. I was angry because he was right, the decision to have an abortion was one that only I could have made. Nobody forced me into anything. But that didn't mean I *wanted* the abortion. I felt sure he was only saying that to make me feel bad, because he was trying to hurt me more. I felt sick to my stomach as I watched Alimu transform from the man I wanted to spend the rest of my life with to a writhing monster who would hurt anyone if it meant he got what he wanted.

"What about my money?" I asked, fearing the answer.

"I had to use it to fix my car. It's your fault I was in a wreck anyway. So, you're going to have to wait for your money," he responded.

I winced at his answer, but what could I say? There was nothing I could do now that would get me my money back, and the ache of being broke just didn't hurt as bad as the ache of being empty. As the hours passed, Alimu would hurl occasional insults my way.

"You're so fat, it's amazing you could find anyone to love you. I like skinny wives."

"You're too big of a whore to make a good mother."

"I'm going to marry you, and then I'm going to cheat on you as much as possible. And I'm going to get all my mistresses pregnant, but I'll never let you get pregnant again."

I knew for sure he was just trying to get me riled up, although I just couldn't understand why he was so insistent on being so cruel. Why was he intentionally trying to hurt me now? Hadn't he done enough already? But I refused to let him have the satisfaction of a reaction. Every insult was met with a low "okay" and nothing more. Perhaps even that was giving him too much. Occasionally, he would hand me back a cigarette. I accepted each offer, although I was confused as to why he was offering to begin with. Still, I didn't want to waste mine if I didn't have to. I'd need to save every last yuan I had. The silence and smoke that filled the car made me suffocate, but I didn't want conversation either. Not with Alimu, not with my friends, and not with my family. I turned off my phone to conserve power and tried my best to sleep the rest of the way back.

We arrived in Xining at around nine-thirty p.m. Alimu drove me back to the hotel where I was staying previously, where Salihan frequented. As he pulled the car over to the curb, he turned around in the driver's seat to face me. As he began talking, I scooted over to the middle back seat, clenched my fist, drew my arm back, and punched him as hard as I could square in the nose. Then I ran as fast as I could out of the car and into the hotel. Before leaving Xining, I'd told the hotel I would be back, and they'd saved my room for me even though I'd handed over my key card. I kept looking over my shoulder as the receptionist re-registered my stay, waiting for Alimu to come inside and hit me back.

I breathed a heavy sigh of relief once I got to my room and closed the door. I needed to pee badly. Alimu hadn't stopped the whole ride down, and my pants were blood-soaked after not being able to change my pad. As I tried to clean myself up a bit, I heard a knock at the door. It was Alimu.

"I need to come in," he said from behind the door.

"Why?" I asked. "What else do you want?"

"I still have to get your train ticket so you can go back to Jinan," he said, then added, "I'm not going to hurt you, Anna."

I opened the door and let him in. He stepped inside, pushing past me, and sat on my bed.

"Why did you hit me?" he said with a truly confused look on his face.

"Because you hurt me," I hissed at him, "so I hurt you back."

Alimu rubbed his face. "That's the first time a woman has ever hit me," he said. I hoped it wouldn't be the last.

I stood over him but said nothing. Suddenly, Alimu cried out and clutched at his stomach. He threw himself back on the bed. "Ugh, it hurts so bad!" he said through clenched teeth, and he curled up in the fetal position, arms wrapped around his abdomen.

"What's wrong?" I asked him.

"My stomach," he responded breathily. "It really hurts."

"Can you stand up?" I asked.

"No, I don't think so, argh!" Alimu winced in pain, writhing on the bed.

"I'm going to call the ambulance," I said, and headed for the door. I wasn't down for playing more games.

"No, wait!" he said, standing up. "I don't need an ambulance. I just need you to stay here with me."

"No, you're having an emergency and you need a doctor," I told him, and started back towards the door.

He slumped to the floor and reached out, grabbing my ankle. "Please, no ambulance. Just sit here with me. I'll get better. I just don't want to be alone right now."

I felt sympathy for him. I knew in my head it wasn't a logical emotion to have for someone who hated me so deeply, and maybe it was just a result of the hormones that still pumped through my body, but I felt legitimate concern. Still, I didn't sit next to him. Rather, I sat on the bed and watched him until he finally seemed to recover from his fit. He then stood up and brushed himself off. Perhaps my lack of a reaction to his crisis bored him.

"I need your passport now," he said. I handed it to him, and he left.

He returned an hour later with my train tickets in hand. He'd purchased a soft sleeper ticket. At least he afforded me that kindness, I thought to myself. He could have saved himself a couple of hundred yuan and purchased a hard seat ticket instead. It wasn't enough to impress me, rather just enough to confuse me. At this point, any kindness Alimu showed me was confusing. Before leaving me for the night, he sat down on the edge of my bed again and asked me to join him.

"Just listen to me," he said in a gentle voice. "I do love you. And I want to be with you, not my wife. I'll call you every other day once you're back in Jinan. And I'll get your money back, too."

"Okay," I responded, not believing a word he said. There was no way I could ever be with him after what he put me through, but even if I wanted him, how could I ever believe him again? I just wanted him out of my room! Thankfully, he stood up after this and left. I checked my train ticket. The departure time was six p.m. the next day. I was relieved that I didn't have to wake up early but disheartened that the train left so late after the hotel checkout time. That meant I would either need to pay for a few extra hours in the hotel or spend the entire afternoon at the train station.

The next afternoon, I opted to pay the hotel's hourly rate. I was still sore from recovery and didn't want to sit in the train station all day. As I transferred my belongings from the overnight rooms to the hourly rooms downstairs, I met one of the housekeepers in the hallway. She smiled at me brightly and asked how the baby was doing. I immediately broke into tears. I told her that I'd had an abortion but then the baby's father told me he was married and left me. She threw down her cleaning supplies and embraced me in her arms. It was the first hug I'd had since leaving Jinan, and it was a hug that I desperately needed. She wiped away my tears and told me, "Things will get better." Then she went back to her work.

I dragged myself through the day and onto the train. Earlier in the train station, I'd met a woman who wanted to add me as a WeChat contact. She was a local journalist, and although we had different seats in different cars, she wanted to get to know me on her trip out of town. I was too mentally tired to say no. Sometimes the easiest thing to do is just say yes. So, I agreed to add her, and we began talking. Of course, she asked me what I was doing in Xining.

I told her that I was pregnant, and that I'd come to find the baby's father's family, to see if they wanted a relationship with the baby or not. I didn't tell her about the abortion. I let her believe that I was still pregnant. I wanted to still be pregnant. I didn't want to have to tell people that I'd had an abortion. I was ashamed and I missed my baby. I felt guilty for missing something that I rejected in the first place, as if I didn't have a right to my grief. I lied through my teeth to that woman, making up almost every aspect of myself. I don't know why I did it. Perhaps it was just to see if I could feel anything again or to see what lying to someone unsuspecting would feel like. I wasn't in a good head space, and I was leaning into my sorrow.

I don't remember who messaged who first, but somewhere a few hours down the track, Micah and I began talking. Micah was a Black man from Harrisburg, Pennsylvania, and a good friend in Jinan. Jinan wasn't used to seeing many Black people. He was one of the most well-read and intellectual individuals I knew, immersing himself in any and every subject of which he could dream. He was a teacher in Jinan, first at an English training school and later for a university. His goal in life was to become a Coptic monk, taking his religion very seriously, yet never throwing it in anyone's face or exposing it without being asked. He was a constant force of goodness in Jinan, a shepherd of comfort, and a serious nerd. Somehow, Micah could sense something was wrong.

"It's been a long time since I've seen you," his message read. "Where are you?"

And so, I told Micah everything. I admitted to him that I'd used my passport as collateral for a massive loan, that Alimu refused to pay me back, that I went on a chase after Yonus, and everything that had happened with Alimu and the abortion. There was a brief silence after I finished my story, and then his reply popped up on my screen.

"Get here," he texted. "You can stay here with me. No, you WILL stay here with me. We're going to get through this together. Anna, don't worry about anything. Just get back to Jinan and we'll go from there."

We formed a plan to meet when my train arrived in Jinan, and he would take me from the railway station to his apartment complex. I turned off my phone to save battery power. I would need it to find Micah, and the power outlet of the sleeper cabin was currently occupied with someone else's charger. I tried to breathe a little—at least when I got to Jinan, I would have a place to stay for a while. I didn't know how long Micah would let me stay, but at least I'd have somewhere to go, and I wouldn't be alone. Plus, Micah agreed to let my cats stay in his apartment, too, and I was eager to see them again, touch their soft fur and hear their cries of joy to see me. At least *they* would be happy to see me. I curled up on the small bed, my face pressed up against the train wall, and slept through most of the journey.

Chapter 27

The train rolled into Jinan well past dark. I expected Micah to meet me in the square in front of the train station, but he wasn't there. Micah was one of the few foreigners who had purchased a large electric scooter for easier travel around the city. He had truly immersed himself in the ways of Jinan traffic and could scuttle about with just as much ease as the locals. His scooter was almost as large as a proper motorcycle with plenty of space for two riders. However, I was concerned about the size and weight of my backpack, and it was a long way from the train station to Micah's apartment.

I called Micah. He was running late. Caught up between the Bible study he led every Wednesday night and the company that a late-night cup of coffee at the local café brought, he found himself still on the east side of the city. He was profusely apologetic and told me to wait for him. I told him not to worry, that if he just gave me the address to his apartment, I could meet him there. In fact, he would probably get there well before I would. He sent over the address and instructed me to wait for him at the gate when I arrived.

It felt overwhelming to be back in Jinan. The sheer expansiveness of the city made Xining feel like a small mountain town, and despite my four years residence in Jinan, I felt like I was stepping foot in the city for the first time. Perhaps it was just me that was different. How could anyone still be the same person after going through what I went through, I thought to myself, then quickly admonished myself for playing the victim. I should have known what Alimu was up to all along. I should have seen the red flags, and looking back, there were plenty, but I got too caught up in wanting that strange and wonderful life with Alimu and lost myself in his abyss.

I was ready to beat myself up for as long as it took for me to feel like I'd fully repented, despite not believing in a punishing god, but I felt my soul needed help. It was burning blue and had donned a layer of char. How could I even face Micah after telling him what I'd done? How could anybody forgive me? Surely, he must think me a fool…

However, when the taxi pulled up in front of Micah's apartment, he was there to greet me with a tight, warm, long embrace. He didn't hate me. He wasn't even ashamed of me, at least not that he showed. He gave me grace and love, which I desperately needed. I shouldered my bag as we began the walk towards his apartment. The building was inside the grounds of a high school. Classrooms made up the north side of the courtyard, while dormitories made up the south side. Micah's apartment building sat to the right of the classrooms. Four stories tall, the building previously housed teachers for the school. Now, it was contracted out by one of the large English training schools as living quarters for its foreign teachers.

Micah's apartment was on the ground floor. I felt a knot grow in my stomach as we reached the entryway to the concrete complex. I knew almost every teacher in this building. Aside from the new recruits, everybody here knew I was pregnant, and I'd solicited several of my friends here for money for Alimu's lorry. I didn't want to face any of them again, but the cold reality was that I'd have to face everyone soon enough. I was dreading trying to explain myself.

The inside of Micah's apartment was simple. Walking in, the large bathroom sat immediately to the left. It was large enough that the western toilet didn't get very wet during showers and the floor in front of the sink stayed mostly dry. I cannot express enough the luxury of a dry bathroom. The living room took up the most space, with two couches, a few low shelves, a coffee table, and a large tv. The kitchen and sunroom sat behind the living room, both behind a sliding glass door. The bedrooms sat to the left of the living room, one on the north side and one on the south side. Micah already occupied the room to the south, so he guided me to the room to the north.

There was a twin bed, a desk, and a dresser. Thankfully, Micah had found sheets, a pillow, and a blanket for me to use for the night. I planned to go to Samm's as soon as possible to pick up the rest of my belongings, including my marital blanket. Micah opened a bottle of wine and found a pair of plastic cups. He handed me the drink as we sat on the couch, and I answered his questions of "how are you" and "what happened" as best as I could. But I was tired, and the night was late. I guzzled the cheap wine and shared a cigarette with Micah. They were black LanZhou's. I loved them, and it was nice to share them with a friend.

The next week was a blur. I managed to get my belongings back from Samm and my cats back from their temporary foster family. Much to Micah's delight, my male cat, Midas, spent the entire week slinking under the kitchen cabinets and yowling to himself. Micah and I soon began yowling at each other, too. Muhaimai still had the majority of my belongings, including my small oven that was a rare treat to own, but Muhaimai was angry at me for having an abortion and told me that if I didn't get my stuff out of his house by the end of the week, he would sell it all. I had no way to get out there, and all of my vitally important belongings were already with me. I was sad to see the belongings that I'd worked so hard to accumulate leave me, but I'd already given up a part of my soul. What were a few measly belongings? I told Muhaimai to sell whatever he wanted, but he should at least keep the oven for himself.

I managed to get in contact with the large English training school I'd worked at before and negotiated a contract with them. It was late October now, and the school was focusing on teaching everyone the choreography to "Thriller" so we could all dance for the parents at the Halloween party. The last thing I wanted to do was dance, but at least I had something to throw myself into. I'd decided to tell the full details of my story to only a select group of friends, those that I felt closest to. So, when my coworkers, expat friends, and local friends alike all asked me about the baby or chastised me for smoking while pregnant, I simply said, "I'm not pregnant anymore," and left it at that. Nobody asked for elaboration, which is what I was counting on.

Micah's training school was constantly recruiting new members, and he quickly became the go-to guy for any and all foreign needs. It was only natural that the teachers were drawn to his charisma and patience, and he knew all the best secrets of Jinan. Micah had an open doors policy in his apartment. Even at night, we rarely locked the doors. If somebody wanted to come in, they were always welcome, day or night, rain or shine. The apartment was rarely empty. It was a safe space for us all.

One new recruit in particular really hit it off with Micah and was in our apartment often. Her name was Priscilla. She was a Jamaican-born citizen who immigrated to Florida as a young woman. Older than most of us in her mid-thirties, Priscilla didn't look a day over twenty-one, and her spirit possessed a youthfulness that made us all want to get to know her better. I instinctively felt comfortable around Priscilla, and it wasn't long before I opened up to her about Alimu. She sat with me through the entire story, and I have a suspicion that she quietly dedicated herself to being my friend after that. Priscilla would become my closest confidante after returning to Jinan. Katherine had returned to the US already, and Samm was busy living her life with her live-in boyfriend. The two of them had become home-bodies, and although Samm's boyfriend was exceedingly wonderful, the three of us rarely got together after my return.

I sank into a deep depression after starting work again. I could barely get myself out of bed. At nights, I would chain smoke cigarettes and drink whatever cheap alcohol I could find, sinking into the mindless English TV shows that Micah had access to on his television. Also, I still had university work to complete. I emailed my professors, informing them that I'd recently lost a baby and was having a hard time coping. They all gave me extensions for my work, but I still felt guilty. I didn't believe I had a right to my grief or the hospitalities my grief afforded me, like extended deadlines. For many nights, I sat on Micah's floor, laptop on the coffee table. I kept a fresh cup of coffee at all times, which had become Micah's and my lifeblood. My ashtray desperately needed emptying, but instead of getting up to walk to the trash can, I would push the ashtray behind my laptop and grab an empty beer bottle instead. Oddly enough, although Micah and I smoked in the apartment quite liberally, our clothes never seemed to stink. Perhaps it was because we always kept our bedroom doors closed and away from the settling smoke. Perhaps we were just blind to the varying scents of China, cigarette smoke being a dominant smell.

On our weekends, Micah and I would walk to the nearest Uni-Mart, a chain of convenience stores with neon green signage that boasted hot food, cold drinks, a small selection of groceries and a large selection of alcohol. Aside from various candy bars and herb crackers, we would buy a two-liter bottle of sweet, pink wine. It held the color and taste of Kool-Aid, but at twelve percent alcohol, it got the job done better than any other spirit we could find within our budget. This wine was literally the cheapest bottle, and we loved it. We named these nights our "wine and tears" nights, when we would sit and talk about our feelings, fears, regrets, and lives in general. I did much more crying than Micah, but it was through these conversations that I learned about Micah's history, his home life, what it was like to be Black in America, and what it was like to be Black in Jinan.

Priscilla would occasionally join us for these nights, too. She would stop in on her way home from dinner, discarding a coat so thick and heavy we playfully called it a small child. Priscilla was not shy about sharing her experiences of being Black in China, and new experiences happened every day. Some encounters were comical, like a coworker telling her that she kept applying chocolate to her skin to try to get it black like Priscilla's (she found Priscilla's skin beautiful, and it was). Others were less pleasant, like being bombarded with streams of people shouting *"hei ren!"* (Black person) as she tried to simply walk down the street. Many members of the Black community in Jinan found safety in Micah's apartment due to their shared experiences and Micah's ability to amplify positivity and a sense of community that was lacking elsewhere around the city.

I found it healthy for me to have a constant stream of people flowing in and out of the apartment. It forced me to be social, to interact with my peers, to get up off the couch, or at least make room for others. Priscilla was known to drag new foreign teachers into Micah's apartment to see me, drawing from my wealth of knowledge of the city, local customs, and language to help make the transition into China-life easier. Some of the new expats took a liking to me immediately. Others took time. One new teacher told me one evening, "they say a lot of bad things about you, but you're the complete opposite of the rumors." That statement cut deeply. I could only imagine what kinds of rumors were flying around about me, and it was true that the extended expat community had been avoiding me lately, acting much less welcoming to me than before I met Alimu. I didn't have the mental bandwidth to pay too much attention to it though. There wasn't anything I could do about it anyway. I was just going to have to let my actions speak for me now.

My actions were illogical, however, and I soon began sleeping during the day and staying up at night until the sun rose. I was melting into liquor bottle after liquor bottle, and my lungs and throat ached from the constant stream of cigarettes. I decided that I needed to take action to save myself. I began scouring the internet for mental health resources for those who had gone through an abortion they regretted. At first, I found nothing that helped, just pages and programs that revolved around forgiveness from Jesus Christ. That wasn't what I was looking for. Eventually, after a week of searching, I stumbled upon a downloadable workbook for post-abortion care.

The workbook acknowledged that abortions happen for many reasons and that feeling guilt, regret, sadness, and grief after an abortion was normal, no matter the reason. I worked through the book page-by-page, some days flying through prompts and thought pieces like cutting soft butter, and other days struggling to make it through the first paragraph of that day's task. Eventually, the workbook suggested naming my lost baby and writing a "goodbye" letter to be read ceremoniously, to represent a funeral. This took the longest time. I wasn't sure what the gender of my baby was, but I'd already had a boy's name picked out just in case: Isiah. And so, I wrote a letter to Isiah and read it aloud to Micah and Priscilla through tears and a shaking voice. In my mind, I placed the letter in a mountain stream and watched it float away, disintegrating into the ether of the Earth. But it still wasn't enough.

Chapter 28

One evening, I received a message from MaJun, Su'erdai's husband.

"Have you heard from Alimu?" he asked me.

"Once," I said. "He called last week to tell me he was getting me my money, but that was it." I didn't believe he was getting me my money anyway. The entire conversation lasted less than a minute.

"I have to tell you something about him," MaJun typed, "but you can't tell anyone else that I told you."

"What is it?" I asked.

"Alimu is married," he said.

"I knew that already," I responded, "but why didn't anyone tell me? Why did everybody keep this a secret from me?"

"I don't know," MaJun said. "You'll have to ask them. But look, he's not just married. He's got two kids from his first marriage, two little girls. And when his ex-wife was pregnant with the youngest one, he got mad at her and dragged her out of bed by her hair. He's not a good person."

Then he continued, "and you're probably never going to get your money back."

After that conversation, something sparked a fire in me. It felt like my soul had reignited, not blazing hot like before, but like its pilot light had been lit again after being extinguished by spilled water. Alimu was awful. I knew that, but he wasn't just awful to me. He was awful to his ex-wife, which meant he was probably awful to his children. And if he was awful to all of us, then he was probably awful to his current wife, too, if she existed. If she didn't, he was bound to be awful to whatever woman would happen to pass his way next. This was an injustice in the world that I couldn't stand for, and I needed to find a way to make it right.

In truth, there weren't many actions I could take that would actually impact Alimu. Except, I thought to myself, if I told on him. Kelimu and Qiong did everything they could to keep me from speaking to his stepfather, and we conveniently never stopped to talk to him before the abortion. All I heard from Alimu and his family were stories about how awful of a man he was, but maybe, just maybe, he would be willing to listen to what I had to say. If I could only get to him, I could tell him everything that was going on. Not just with Alimu, but with his whole family. After all, it wasn't just Alimu that had deceived me. Each of his siblings had played a role in this. At any point, any of them could have told me the truth about Alimu, and I would have been spared from this pain. Now, I said to myself, it was time to repay that pain.

I still had Alimu's address from the photo of his license that I recovered from my phone's trash folder, and I already knew how to get there. All I needed now was a way back out to Xining then northwest to YangLong. I decided not to reach out to my karaoke group this time. They had already done plenty for me, and in truth, I was embarrassed that I'd let myself be fooled by Alimu. I didn't want to admit to them how everything turned out. However, I was still keeping casual conversation with XiaoTong, the noodle-puller from MenYuan. I asked him if he knew of a way to find a driver to take me to YangLong and how much the journey would cost.

"My boss can drive you there," XiaoTong responded. "All you need to do is get to MenYuan."

"Thank you, XiaoTong," I said, "and please tell your boss I said thank you, too. How much will I owe him?"

"Don't worry about it," XiaoTong said. "You're a friend in need, so I've got that covered."

It was a perfect example of the kindness that Chinese people would afford you once they considered you a friend. It didn't matter if you were a friend for just a few weeks or a friend from a lifetime ago. Going out of one's way to help a friend was just what folks did. However, looking back I wonder again if XiaoTong's willingness to help me wasn't due in part to the fact that I was a foreigner. Still, getting out to MenYuan would not be an easy task. I needed to get to Xining first, and from there I'd have to figure out how to get into HaiBei County again without being noticed by the police. The latter had never been a problem in the past, but it was something that sat in the back of my mind on every excursion I'd made out west.

This time, I told everybody about my plan. The last time I did something extraordinary, I kept it to myself and ended up in trouble. I would not let that happen again. I needed solid heads and sturdy hearts to follow me where I was going, even if they weren't there physically. Looking up train tickets, I found the only ones left were standing room only for the next two weeks. I wasn't going to wait two weeks. I wanted this done immediately. Perhaps my depression had swung upwards into mania, or perhaps my heart was just too hardened for me to bear anymore. Maybe I couldn't stand up for two days straight, but I sure could sit on the floor! Moreover, the train might not be completely full forever. It was sometimes possible to upgrade your tickets after boarding the train, even if just for a few stops.

I shoved a week's worth of clothes into my backpack. I could wear some outfits more than once, following the local customs, so long as I changed my socks and underwear every day. I filled what little room I had left in my bag with snacks and water for the trip and somehow convinced work to give me the time off. Then I found a notebook and began to write. I wrote down everything that had happened between Alimu, his siblings, and myself, starting from meeting Alimu online. It was a long and complicated story, and I needed to get the Chinese down and practice some of the words before trying to explain it all to Alimu's stepfather. I wrote the characters and the pinyin (phonetic pronunciation) alike, in chronological order, including dates and times and as many details as I could remember. I had to reorganize my bag to make the notebook fit, but it was the key to a successful mission.

The next morning, I woke up early. The train would leave before noon, so I had enough time to dawdle, but I was ready to go from the moment I woke up. Micah and Priscilla said goodbye and wished me luck, then I headed to the train station. Soon, I stood on the platform and watched the train pull in, ticket inspectors deboarding to welcome new passengers. My train car was the second to last car on the tracks, and the ticket inspector looked unhurried. I approached him and showed him my ticket. I asked if there were any seats or sleepers available for shorter stretches. His eyes widened and he gasped when he saw my ticket.

"A standing ticket to Xining?" he asked.

"It was the only ticket they had left, and I really need to get out there," I responded.

"Let me see what I can do," he said. "That's too uncomfortable for such a long ride."

He waved a hand for me to follow him, and we walked up the platform towards the dining car where he showed another crew member my ticket. Her eyes also widened when she saw my ticket.

"Come with me," she said, and she led me to the dining car.

"You can't sit in here just yet, so you'll have to either stand or sit right outside," she explained, "but when the dining car opens, you can pay for a meal and sit there as long as you like."

"But," she went on to say, "you have to keep paying for meals. Breakfast, lunch, and dinner. Anytime a meal is offered, you have to pay for it if you want to keep sitting there, and seats are severely limited. I'll make sure you get a spot."

I thanked her for helping me and sat down on the dirty train car floor. A scrap of cardboard lay next to me, a remnant of the previous passenger who could also only sit. I hastily grabbed it up, sliding it under my own rump to keep from ruining my pants with grime and mud. The train was absolutely packed, and I wasn't the only one vying for a seat in the dining car. Three hours passed before the dining car was officially opened, and once it was, everyone jumped and pushed and shoved for seats. I was about to sit down, when a man pushed past me at the very last second, taking my seat. I protested heavily.

"I was just about to sit there! You could clearly see me!" I cried.

"But I got it first. It's not my fault you were too slow," he said.

"No, that's not fair," I shouted at him, "I waited my turn just like everybody else here, and you have no right to push me away when my ass was practically already in the seat. You weren't even waiting with the rest of us!"

I was fuming. I was shouting. Soon two crew members made their way over to ask what was going on. We both gave our version of events, and the crew member that had assisted me earlier made the man give up his seat for me. All eyes of the dining car were on me as I took the aisle seat of the four-person booth. I shoved my face into my book, cheeks burning hot with embarrassment, and waited for our meal to be served. At thirty yuan per meal, we all paid a surcharge for the privilege of sitting in the dining car. While the cost was certainly on the high end of what one might pay for a meal in China, it didn't feel *too* expensive, at least not at first, but my bank roll was still extremely thin as I had only been working again for less than a month. The cost of all the meals across 42 hours added up fast.

There were three other people in the booth with me, all men. The people across the aisle were also all men. They were all intrigued by my hair at first and then wanted to know where I was going and why. I told them I was off to Xining to get my money back from an ex-boyfriend, and they all called me *niu bi* (basically a badass) and wished me luck. I didn't mention anything about the pregnancy or resulting abortion. I still couldn't talk about it without breaking down inside. Afterwards, I tried to read my book as much as possible but found it difficult to concentrate. I'd taken the book of short stories with me again. I thought the familiarity of the stories would be comforting, but instead I found the predictability frustrating and focused more on getting to the end of a story rather than truly ingesting the words.

It was harder to sleep in the dining car booths but not impossible. At night, heads found their neighbor's shoulders despite being strangers, and those with enough space slumped over on the tables, straining their backs and necks for a few hours of rest. I was lucky enough to have room to slide part of my backpack up on the table and use it as a pillow. The crew members made us buy a midnight snack in order to stay there for the night. By the time we reached Xining, most of the original members of the mad rush to the dining car had deboarded at other stations, and I was now surrounded by new strangers who had no interest in speaking to me. That was okay, though, because I didn't really want to speak to anybody either.

As the train rolled into the Xining station, I was playing through my options for my next steps in my head. There were a few ways I could get to MenYuan from Xining. The first option was the bullet train, which was only a thirty-minute ride, but I would need to pass through multiple officer checkpoints and might be easily noticed. This wasn't the most expensive option, but it also wasn't the cheapest. The second option was a bus. It was a three-hour drive to MenYuan, which meant that a long-distance bus would likely take closer to four hours, as they drove at significantly slower speeds. This was the cheapest option, but still held some risk of being noticed by someone who would know I shouldn't be there. My third option was to hire a private driver to make the trip. This would be the most secure option but also the most expensive, and it wasn't guaranteed that I could find somebody willing to drive me there right away.

I decided to try my luck with the buses and made my way to the bus station, which was only a five-minute taxi ride away. I purchased tickets without issue and without needing to show my passport. I still had an hour and a half before the bus would leave, so I took the opportunity to smoke a few LanZhou cigarettes. My heart pounded when it was time to board the bus. I thought for sure someone would grab me at any second and pull me out of line, informing me that foreigners can't go where I was headed, but nobody said anything or even looked my way for more than a second. I took a window seat at the back of the bus and hunkered down low. The tops of my dreadlocks were still peeking out above the headrest, but at least my white and foreign face was concealed.

The journey into MenYuan was uneventful, although I greatly enjoyed traveling up and over the mountains again, seemingly teetering on the backs of the ridges that snaked through the land. XiaoTong met me at the town center, where the bus finally came to a stop. We first grabbed lunch together and ate heartily. Then, XiaoTong led me to a hotel across the street.

"It's too late to leave today," he said, "so you can stay here for the night. I've already booked your room."

"How much was it? I'll pay you back," I told him.

"No," he insisted. "You can't even get your own hotel room here, or else you'll get in trouble. And besides, I already paid."

"All right," I said, "but let me pay for dinner." XiaoTong agreed.

XiaoTong had to go back to work after receiving me, so I stayed in the hotel room alone, taking the opportunity to touch base with Micah and Priscilla. XiaoTong told me that his boss would visit me after work, and we would work out the finer details of our trip for tomorrow. His boss arrived around 9:30pm, after his noodle shop closed. When I opened my hotel door for him, he came in and immediately laid down in my bed. He lit up a cigarette and told me that it would cost me five hundred yuan for the trip and that he needed to pick up someone else on the way. I felt uncomfortable with this man, and he leered at me with an unmistakable look of lust. I wanted him out of my hotel room. He continued to lie on my bed until he finished his cigarette, then he tamped it out directly on the bedside table and left.

I messaged XiaoTong and told him that I didn't feel comfortable with his boss. XiaoTong immediately went into a rage.

"What do you mean, he laid in your bed?" he questioned. "That's unforgivable! I can't believe he would do that to you!"

The way his boss behaved was a major cultural faux pas for the Hui, and it made us both feel uneasy. This was a big deal to XiaoTong.

"I'm not working for a pervert anymore," he said. "I'm quitting!"

So, he quit his job on the spot. I urged him not to do that, especially not on my behalf, but he said it wasn't about me. It was about the morality of his boss, and if he couldn't trust his boss to act accordingly towards me, he couldn't trust him in business either.

He sent a smiling emoji and wrote, "Now that I don't have a job, I can figure out a better way to get you to YangLong! I'll see you in the morning, okay? I'll be there at 6:00am, so make sure you wake up early!"

I slept well that night despite not knowing tomorrow's plan. It was a relief to not have to ride with XiaoTong's boss, and I felt that if XiaoTong was so appalled by his actions, then I probably wasn't wrong in my assessment of him either.

Chapter 29

XiaoTong knocked on the hotel door at exactly six a.m. He was nothing but smiles.

"Are you ready for breakfast?" he asked.

"I'm starving!" I replied, and followed XiaoTong outside to catch a cab.

To my surprise, we didn't head to a restaurant, but rather to the outskirts of town, where the apartments ended and the villages began. There, XiaoTong introduced me to his friend, MaGe. MaGe was older, in his late fifties or early sixties, with snow white hair and crow's feet around the eyes. He stood slightly hunched as he introduced himself and gestured for us to follow him inside his home.

He motioned for me to have a seat on his *kang*, a common type of large, raised concrete bed in rural areas where winters are harsh. Fires are lit under the beds to keep them warm throughout the night, and during the day, *kangs* are used as sitting and entertainment areas. He and XiaoTong left for the kitchen and were gone for quite some time, but he brought me a bowl of fresh milk, squeezed from the cow earlier that morning, with a layer of fat skimming the surface. It was warm and silky and paired perfectly with the assortment of breads that MaGe had laid out for breakfast.

"Once you're done eating, MaGe will take you to YangLong," said XiaoTong, "but he wants to know if you can cover hotel expenses. He can't make it there and back in one day. But two hundred yuan should be plenty. Do you have it?"

I did. That amount I could part with, but not much more. I wasted no time getting ready to leave, stuffing my mouth with one last bite of bread and taking a big gulp of milk to wash it down. Then MaGe and I loaded up in his car and started driving. It was shortly after seven o'clock when we left, and the journey took us nearly ten hours. The drive itself was uneventful, and MaGe and I didn't speak, except to confirm that the other needed to stop for the restroom or to eat. We arrived in YangLong a little past five p.m., and after I directed MaGe where to turn, I stepped out of the car mere feet from Alimu's house. I said my goodbyes to MaGe, shouldered my backpack, and walked into the courtyard.

A young boy of maybe five years was playing outside. He saw me coming, and once my feet planted over the courtyard threshold, he went running into the house. I kept walking. The front door to the sunroom was wide open and I stepped inside. Immediately to my left, Alimu's mother moved from one room to the other.

"Hello! Do you remember me?" I asked her.

She shook her head violently and quickly pushed past me.

I turned to enter the room she had just come from and found three men, two sitting on the *kang* and one sitting in a wooden chair. Between them was a picked-over boiled goat's head, which was considered a delicacy in this area. Its eyes were still intact as the men plucked the flesh from its skull. They looked up at me as I approached, and immediately one of them spoke.

"Please, sit down!" he said, and motioned to another wooden chair.

"I'm looking for Alimu's father," I began, but was interrupted.

"Sit, sit!" said the man. "Drink some tea!"

I was a total stranger that had just walked into this man's home. A foreign stranger at that, who couldn't speak the dialect and had weird hair, and the first thing he said to me was not "what are you doing in my house", but rather "please sit and have some tea". This was another testament to the importance of proper hospitality. I sat as requested. Then I spoke again.

"I'm looking for Alimu's father," I said, heart racing and hands shaking, "or MaNai's father."

One of the men's eyes widened at my statement. I turned to him and asked him, "Are you Alimu's father?" He shook his head.

The taller man sitting on the *kang* pointed a finger at his chest.

"That's me," he said. With that, his guests stood up and left, saying the briefest of goodbyes before departing.

I began by apologizing for barging into his house unannounced.

"But there's something I really want to tell you," I said, "and I hope that you'll listen. It's a long story, and my Chinese isn't good enough for all of it, but please listen."

Then I opened my bag and retrieved my notebook. Turning halfway through the book, I found the pages where I had written out the timeline of events. I told him everything. I was nervous, and my voice wavered and cracked as I spoke. At times, I wiped away tears. Alimu's stepfather listened intently, leaning his body further and further over to the table with each new event I spoke about. He put his hand over his mouth, lowered his eyes, and listened. When I was finished, he stood up and walked over to me.

Peering down at me, he said, "I can't get your money back, and I can't make him marry you. He's a bad person. You don't want to marry him anyway. You got lucky, really, that you're no longer involved with him."

I told him that I understood about the money. I didn't think he personally had any to give, and although I was hoping and praying that Alimu would pay me back, I wasn't counting on it anymore.

"Why did you come here?" Alimu's stepfather asked me.

"Because I've been hurt and I needed somebody to know," I replied.

Alimu's stepfather nodded his head. "You wait here," he said. "He'll have to face the consequences!"

With that, he took out his phone and walked outside. I watched from the window and heard him yelling "Kelimu" through the panes. Then he hung up and made another phone call. There was no answer. He tried again, and again no answer. He made another call and was on *this* call for a long time. Then he came back inside.

"Kelimu is refusing to come home, and Yonus isn't picking up his phone," he said, "but Alimu is on his way here."

I nodded and he exited the room, walking towards where his wife had scampered off to. She came to me a few minutes later with hot tea and poured me a glass. The two of them talked between themselves, lowly arguing, while Alimu's father continued to make a series of phone calls. I couldn't tell who they were to or what they were about, however, due to the *Qinghai Hua* that everyone else but me spoke.

It was well before nightfall, but I was feeling drowsy. Maybe it was the altitude, but my eyelids soon drooped from exhaustion, and I couldn't keep my head from nodding.

"Are you sleepy?" Alimu's mother asked me.

"I'm so sorry," I told her. "I'm trying to stay awake, but I guess I'm just tired."

"Come, we have a spare room where you can sleep," she said, and she grabbed me by the arm and led me into the second bedroom. This bedroom had no *kang*, just a metal framed bed and stiff mattress, but it was comfortable enough to lay down on. Alimu's mother brought me a few blankets and told me not to worry about sleeping too long. It would be hours before Alimu got here. Reluctantly, I drifted off to sleep.

I awoke with a jolt. It was dark now, and there were no lights on in the room. I stumbled out into the main sitting room, where Alimu's stepfather sat on the *kang* and his mother sat on a small couch beside the bed. The little boy from earlier played with the frills on her shirt.

"This is Yonus' son," she told me.

I tried to tell him hello, but he buried his face into his grandmother. She smiled and chuckled. Soon, Alimu's stepfather's phone rang, and he excused himself to answer it.

"This poor child," said Alimu's mother. "It's past his bedtime, but you're here, so he's staying up."

I didn't know how to respond.

"You already had the abortion," she continued, "so why make all this fuss, huh? Why not just let the past be the past? You can't change anything now." Her tone was condescending.

Before I could answer her, Alimu's stepfather returned.

"Alimu will be here in an hour," he said.

Chapter 30

The first thing Alimu did when he walked through his front door and into the sitting room was grab my glass of tea and throw it in my face. Flowers and tea leaves stuck to my hair as water dripped down my cheeks and soaked my shirt. Luckily, it had been sitting for a while and was only lukewarm. His mother jumped up, hissed at him sharply, then began picking the flowers and leaves from my hair. Alimu clenched his teeth and turned his lips up in a snarl. He opened his mouth, surely about to spit out the most vile words he could muster, but he was cut off by his stepfather who had just reentered the room.

His mother quickly exited, and Alimu backed away from him. His stepfather didn't shout but spoke in a calm and even tone. I had no clue as to what he was saying but watched as Alimu continued to slowly back away until he bumped against the *kang*, folded his arms around his body, and shifted his gaze to his feet. His stepfather spoke for ten minutes straight, occasionally pointing a finger at Alimu or gesturing wildly, but never raising his voice. Then, Alimu began to cry. Tears rolled down his cheeks, although he didn't make a sound.

When his stepfather was done, Alimu walked past him silently, headed towards his mother in the back room. His stepfather didn't say a word to me but walked to his *kang* and sat down. I stared at him and wanted to speak, but before I could open my mouth, I noticed a motion from the corner of my eyes. It was Alimu's mother. She waved me back to join her, making big sweeping motions with her arms.

"Excuse me," I said as I stood up and exited the room.

Alimu, his mother, and Yonus's son were all in the back room, with Yonus's son curled up asleep on a *kang*. Alimu spoke to me in a harsh whisper.

"You're a fucking bitch for coming here," he said.

"I am," I said coldly, and stared at him.

"My wife is having a miscarriage–" he began, but before he could finish his sentence, I lunged at him, scratching his face with my nails, and leaving visible marks.

He screamed at me, "My face! Look what you've done to my face!"

"I'll do more," I told him through gritted teeth.

"Oh, my poor son!" his mother shouted and cradled his head in her hands. She held her arm out in my direction to keep me away from him. I stood there, seething at him, saying nothing.

Alimu checked his face in a mirror, complaining about a drop of blood he squeezed through a scratch. Then he turned to me.

"Go and tell my stepfather that you're leaving. I'm taking you back to Xining," he said.

"Why would I go anywhere with you?" I asked him.

"Because my stepfather ordered me to make sure you got back safely," he said. "Now go!"

At this point, I wasn't sure that there was any other alternative. I'd completed the mission I set out to do, speaking to Alimu's stepfather, telling him everything that had happened. I wouldn't be getting any money back, and whatever went on between him and his stepfather, it was enough to make him cry. If I waited around until morning, the police would probably show up to escort me out of the county, as word travels fast in small towns, especially when a foreigner is involved. So, I walked back to the room where Alimu's stepfather was sitting and gathered my belongings.

Alimu's stepfather stared at me but said nothing.

"Thank you for listening to me," I told him.

"Are you leaving?" he asked, but before I could respond, Alimu pushed past me and began speaking with him. I turned out of the room and stepped out into the courtyard, bypassing a curious goat that was attempting to gain entry into the sunroom. I looked up to find a cloudy sky. There would be no blanket of stars tonight.

"Let's go," Alimu said sternly as he exited the house and made his way to the car.

I sat in the front passenger seat.

"Sit in the back," he told me.

"No," I responded. "I'm sitting right here."

I didn't budge, and Alimu didn't push again. It was late, well past ten o'clock, and we were going to have a long night.

An hour later, Alimu broke the silence in the car.

"Are you happy now?" he asked.

"Yes, I'm happy," I said coldly.

"Really? You're happy right now?" he persisted.

"I'm happier than I was a week ago, yeah!" I barked at him.

"Do you know what my stepfather did to me?" he said calmly. "He banned me from the house. I'm not allowed to go back ever again. Qiong and Kelimu's ceremonial marriage has been called off, and Yonus's son isn't allowed to live with them anymore."

"Oh," I said. "That's good."

"That's good?" Alimu shouted. "You've ruined my life!"

"Just like you ruined mine!" I shouted back, then fell silent, but Alimu began hurling insults and calling me names.

"Oh, fuck this," I said, and reached for the car door handle. "Stop the car!"

"What are you doing?" he cried out. "You can't get out here!"

"And why not?" I asked.

"Because there are ghosts out here!" he said in an exasperated tone.

I stared at him momentarily before reaching for the door handle again.

"How are you going to get home?" Alimu asked.

"I don't know," I said. "I'll walk if I have to, but I can't stand another minute in the car with you."

"You can't go back there," he said. "My stepfather welcomed you in his home once, but he won't welcome you again. Don't bother them. Just get back in the car."

He was probably right. I had nowhere to go, and attempting to walk back to YangLong in the middle of the night with absolutely no light source in what was literally the middle of nowhere was a bad idea. I sat back in the car, and Alimu handed me a cigarette. As we headed down the road once more, I contemplated the nature of smoking culture in China, and how even in times of extreme pain and hatred, that same culture still drove Alimu to politely offer me a smoke. I decided to offer him one of my cigarettes an hour later, just to see if he would take it out of obligation. He did. Then my experiment was over, and I sank into my head again.

Alimu pulled over to the side of the road around three-thirty a.m.

"I want you to sit in the back seat," he said.

"I already told you I'm going to sit right here," I replied.

"No," he responded. "I'm going to get some sleep now. You can lay down in the back seat and sleep too."

That sounded like a good idea. I didn't want a sleepy driver, and staying awake all night served no purpose. So, I lay in the backseat, using my backpack as a pillow and my coat as a blanket. Alimu leaned his driver's seat as far back as he could and fell asleep. I soon heard him snoring softly, but I struggled to find rest. I slept on and off for four hours, but with the sun already risen and burning brightly through the car windows, it was hard to stay asleep. I kept hoping Alimu would wake up. I stepped out of the car to smoke again and watched two cars pass by. They were the only other cars we'd seen since leaving YangLong. I sent text messages to Micah and Priscilla, updating them on my situation. Then my empty stomach began to complain about not being properly fed for the past two days.

I climbed back in the car and shook Alimu awake.

"Let's go," I said. "It's morning."

"Let me sleep," he said. "I'm too tired for this."

"I'm hungry," I told him.

"Then smoke a cigarette," he replied. "I'm not stopping anywhere." Then he rolled to his left side and let out a huff of air.

I smoked another cigarette outside and picked through the rocks on the side of the road. They were large and smooth, leftover glacial deposits from long ago. I pocketed a couple of the prettiest ones I could find, one in the shape of a heart. Then Alimu stepped out of the car. He leaned against the car door and stretched, then lit up a smoke. We said nothing to each other. I watched as he chucked the butt of his cigarette into the sedges then opened his car door again.

Alimu called out to me.

"Anna!" he said. "Please sit in the back seat. I really don't want to look at you."

Whatever, I thought to myself, and decided this wasn't the hill to die on. I took the back seat. Now, I have a suspicion that the reason he didn't want me in the front seat was because he didn't want any passing drivers to see us together. The only other fellow motorists would be other village natives. I have no evidence to back up this suspicion. It is just a hunch, albeit a very strong one.

The drive back into Xining was long but uneventful. Alimu and I chain-smoked all our cigarettes, and in the back seat, I felt myself relax a little. I tried to let the tension flow out of my body and focus on the surrounding mountain views, full of snow caps and herds of yak. We were silent now. Alimu had tried asking me awful questions and telling me awful things, but I either refused to answer or told him "I don't care," and he was bored of his unsuccessful attempts to goad a reaction from me.

Arriving in Xining, Alimu drove to the front of the same salmon colored hotel that he took me to the first time we came to Xining together.

"No," I told him. "I can't do this. Not here."

"Then tell me where you want to go," he said.

I sat in the car for a moment and thought to myself, "you're strong enough to do this, Anna, it's okay," and told him that I'd changed my mind, that this was fine.

"Well then... how do you say it in English..." he paused then gestured to my door with his hand and said, in English, *"please."* I opened the car door to leave, but before I left, I turned once more to Alimu.

"Maybe we can still be friends," I snarled at him sarcastically. He twisted his face into a look of anger and disgust. I got out of the car, closed the door, and walked away. That was the last time I ever saw Alimu.

I walked into the hotel, paid for a room, and tried to purchase train tickets online, but I just couldn't do it. Despite my inner pep talk, I couldn't stay in that hotel that housed so many memories for me. Not even half an hour after checking in, I checked back out and made my way back to the more familiar hotel near Salihan's work. That hotel felt more like a base camp than anything else, and returning there at the end felt like truly closing a chapter.

I managed to snag a bottom bunk hard sleeper ticket for the train ride home to Jinan. Boarding the train, I was overall poorer in pocket, but richer in heart. I felt validated. I felt vindicated. I felt like I might be able to forgive myself and move on. Maybe I would never be able to forgive Alimu, and I certainly would never forget him, but as I slumped my backpack down onto the sleeper bed and sat down for the long journey home, I breathed a heavy sigh of relief, knowing that this chapter of my life was finally... closed.

Epilogue

After returning to Jinan, I continued to live with Micah for quite some time. We greatly enjoyed each other's company, concocting new adventures and exploring the minds of our fellow expats with our open doors policy. But Jinan was rapidly changing, growing its economic power and outward expansion by the day, and the mountains of Qinghai had truly stolen my heart. I moved out to Xining the following summer and found a job teaching at a local kindergarten.

MaJun would later contact me demanding to know if I had told Alimu that he'd tipped me off about his marriage and children. Somehow, they had figured it out, and as a result, Su'erdai left him. I attempted briefly to get answers from his siblings, but they all blocked me, except for Su'erdai. She told me she was obligated to help him since he was her brother, although she swore that she didn't know what Alimu was up to when he planned the abortion. I tried to ask why she didn't tell me he was married or even if he truly *was* married and if he'd really been banned from the family house, but all she would respond with was "I don't want to talk about Alimu." I still haven't let go of wanting to know all the answers, but I gave up on trying to find them well before moving to Xining.

I cut my dreadlocks as well. Not because the hairstyle was a negative force in my life, but because I felt I was writing a new chapter in a new book and a brand-new Anna needed brand new hair. Micah commiserated with me as we took scissors to the locks, less than two inches of freestanding hair left of my head. I gathered the locks into a big pile, gifted some to the weird and wonderful friends who requested a bodily souvenir, and kept my favorite ones with me until I left China. At that point, I'd been in the country for five years and was ready to truly return home.

Zhen moved back to his native village in Henan where he opened his own construction business. He is mildly successful and misses hairdressing but can't afford to change careers. Samm went on to marry her Chinese boyfriend, and they now live together near her parents in New York. They own both a dog and a massage parlor. Katherine surprisingly moved to my neck of the woods in Indiana and now lives an hour's drive from me. She prides herself on her social work with Native American tribes and her lithography. Micah now lives in Egypt, where he can be close to his Coptic community. He still hopes to become a monk. Priscilla went on to become a teacher in Florida. She is the godmother of both of my children (yes, I am happily married with kids now), and we vacation together regularly.

As for Alimu, he now owns a business selling cordyceps, rare mushrooms, and saffron as high-dollar gifts exclusively from the Qinghai-Tibetan Plateau. He regularly posts videos of himself on social media, sifting through massive piles of caterpillar fungus. I know this because I never deleted him from my WeChat contacts, and I can still see the public posts for his business. I tried to reach out to him exactly once, two years after leaving China. He simply told me "I don't know you," and blocked me from his chats. I will admit to still keeping track of his contact and business information, although it comes from a place of anger and desire to know thy enemy. Perhaps it is my way of proving that I still have control. I did learn from Salihan, who met me in Xining and told me "I tried to warn you," that Alimu did not cut off his own finger. Rather, it was the result of a loan shark that Alimu was late to repay.

During the two day's train ride back to Jinan, I made the conscious decision to not let my experience with Alimu harden my heart. My options were to either let everything that happened turn my heart into stone, darken my soul, and compel me to live in anger and fear of the world, or I could choose the path of compassion, grace, and empathy. I decided to take the latter. Something good needed to come from this, and I was determined to turn my rage into warmth and light. I now make it a point to be a source of comfort and understanding to those around me.

I regret my decision to have an abortion, although I do feel it was the right decision to make. After some intensive therapy and evaluation of the type of person that Alimu was, I strongly believe that if I hadn't agreed to have the abortion, he would have killed me on that mountain. And I believe his siblings would have helped him cover it up. Nobody knew I was up there. Nobody was checking on me to make sure I was okay, and nobody would have ever thought to look in the hillsides of YangLong to find a missing foreigner. I believe he would have strangled me in the tent or found the heavy and burning tea kettle from inside. I don't believe I would have survived if I'd not agreed to the abortion, so therefore, it was the right overall choice.

Alimu was a clinical psychopath, and perhaps a narcissist. I often wonder how many other women's doorways he has darkened, and, knowing that he is married now, I pray that his wife is safe. I think about Isiah less and less these days, although late Octobers generally find me glum, but I am grateful for the children I have now, and I aim to be the mom for them that I couldn't be for my first. Overall, I am appalled by the lack of mental health care available for women who have had abortions in the United States, as I have spoken with many others with similar stories, and all found themselves in desperate need of a way to work through their grief. But I am mostly grateful for the love and compassion my friends and family have shown me as I spend my years picking up the remaining broken pieces of my soul that Alimu shattered. I've learned that shattered souls can be fixed, and when lovingly polished, they shine like stained glass.

About The Author

Anna Keibler is a professional writer, youth worker, and traveler with a fervent passion for languages, art, and wildlife. As a nature lover with a master's in natural resources, she has a passion for the ecological conservation of the Qinghai-Tibetan Plateau.

Originally hailing from rural Indiana, Anna learned Mandarin after living and working in China for more than five years. With more than a decade of experience in teaching English, essay writing, and research strategies, she has built a strong foundation of creative writing experience in the nonfiction space.

In her spare time, Anna can often be found crafting, adventuring, enjoying Chinese folk music, and scouring either the night sky for unusual astral phenomena or her backyard for natural herbal remedies.

Note From Anna Keibler

Word-of-mouth is crucial for any author to succeed. If you enjoyed *A Ghost in the Middle Kingdom,* please leave a review online—anywhere you are able. Even if it's just a sentence or two. It would make all the difference and would be very much appreciated.

Thanks!
Anna Keibler

We hope you enjoyed reading this title from:

www.blackrosewriting.com

Subscribe to our mailing list – *The Rosevine* – and receive **FREE** books, daily deals, and stay current with news about upcoming releases and our hottest authors.
Scan the QR code below to sign up.

Already a subscriber? Please accept a sincere thank you for being a fan of Black Rose Writing authors.

View other Black Rose Writing titles at www.blackrosewriting.com/books and use promo code **PRINT** to receive a **20% discount** when purchasing.

www.ingramcontent.com/pod-product-compliance
Lightning Source LLC
Chambersburg PA
CBHW072155070526
44585CB00015B/1153